THE AMERICAN CORPORATE NETWORK

Volume 138, Sage Library of Social Research

RECENT VOLUMES IN
SAGE LIBRARY OF SOCIAL RESEARCH

THE **AMERICAN CORPORATE NETWORK**
1904-1974

Mark S. Mizruchi

Foreword by **G. William Domhoff**

Volume 138
SAGE LIBRARY OF
SOCIAL RESEARCH

SAGE PUBLICATIONS Beverly Hills London

Copyright © 1982 by Sage Publications, Inc.

For information address:

SAGE Publications, Inc.
275 South Beverly Drive
Beverly Hills, California 90212

SAGE Publications India Pvt. Ltd.
C-236 Defence Colony
New Delhi 110 024, India

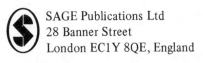

SAGE Publications Ltd
28 Banner Street
London EC1Y 8QE, England

Printed in the United States of America

Library of Congress Cataloging in Publication Data

Mizruchi, Mark S.
   The American corporate network, 1904-1974.

   (Sage library of social research ; v. 138)
   Includes bibliographical references.
   1. Corporations--United States--History--
20th century. I. Title. II. Series.
HD2785.M57   338.7'4'0973   81-18477
ISBN 0-8039-1778-3   AACR2
ISBN 0-8039-1779-1 (pbk.)

FIRST PRINTING

CONTENTS

For Katherine

FOREWORD

This closely argued and highly informative study of the patterns created by shared corporate directorships in the American business community marks a turning point in an area of interest within both power structure research and organizational sociology that has a long past and a short, intense history.

Although the book itself is about a formal and public network that can be traced out from listings in Standard and Poor's *Register of Corporations, Directors and Executives,* the basis for the study is in one of those informal networks or "invisible colleges" through which so much scientific work takes place. In that sense, the book is a testimony to the great sense of community and sharing that came to exist in the 1970s among a group of people working in different parts of the country who spent many tedious and often frustrating hours compiling data bases, perfecting new quantitative measures, and reworking computer programs.

But the book is not only a culmination of a sustained research effort that has been centered among sociologists at the State University of New York at Stony Brook, with a large assist from economist David Bunting of Eastern Washington State University. It is also a beginning, for it demonstrates to even the most skeptical of social science readers that there are meaningful patterns in corporate interlock data, something that has been doubted again and again throughout decades of one-shot efforts that often produced somewhat contradictory results.

The data base for this book is a deceptively simple one. It consists of a list of people's names followed by their corporate affiliations. But in fact this people-to-groups matrix embodies both levels of social relationships of concern to social scientists, interpersonal relations and interorganizational networks. The tracing of people and their affiliations in a rigorous way, which sometimes appears suspect to critics of power structure research, encompasses fundamental levels of sociological theorizing. Sociologist Ronald Breiger (in an article entitled "The Duality of Persons and Groups," *Social Forces,* December 1974) reminded his colleagues of this in a persuasive demonstration of the potential importance of fully understanding what he calls the "duality of persons and groups" by means of "membership network analysis."

To report any of the many new findings of this book here would be to take away some of the fun of reading this rich and informative account, so I will instead close by asking readers to keep in mind that the possibilities exist for even further breakthroughs in this area. For example, the information is available for extending the network data base back to at least the early 1880s, thanks to the efforts of Bunting and sociologist William Roy, and work by sociologist Elizabeth Sholes is under way that might carry it back to the early part of that century. Moreover, there is the basis (in data compiled by political scientist Thomas Dye and sociologist Harold Salzman for the years 1969-1970) for including other organizations that are part of this business-based network—law firms, foundations, think tanks, and policy groups; and there are private school alumni lists, club membership lists, social registers, and even attitude and opinion data for those years as well.

However, a claim about possibilities should not lead to the thought that future results will come easily or all at once. I can remember clearly that in 1970-1971, when the invisible college around this issue began to form, it seemed as if great strides would be made in no time flat. The ensuing ten years showed that progress would be much slower than we had hoped. There are endless technical problems, and the number of quantitatively oriented social scientists who are willing to deal with the taboo topic of corporate power remains small.

The appearance of this book rekindles earlier hopes. It fulfills the promise of all this work by so many hands. May the invisible college created by Michael Schwartz, Peter Mariolis, and others at SUNY—Stony Brook in 1970-1971 continue to exist, and may many more fine young social scientists such as Mark Mizruchi feel free to join it, wherever they may be.

G. William Domhoff
University of California—Santa Cruz

PREFACE

This book is part of a larger research project, the aim of which is to understand the structure of power in American society. I first became interested in this topic as an undergraduate at Washington University. While canvassing Democratic neighborhoods in South St. Louis during the 1972 presidential campaign, I was perplexed by the conservatism of many of the working-class people with whom I spoke. This curiosity led me to the study of sociology, where I became engrossed in questions of how social order is maintained, and "who rules America." During my second year in graduate school at SUNY–Stony Brook, I took a seminar in political sociology with Michael Schwartz. That semester (spring 1977) I attended a colloquium on corporate ownership and control presented by Beth Mintz, then one of Schwartz's students. I had always found this topic intriguing, but, like many others, I wasn't sure why the issue was important. This presentation for the first time illuminated for me the relation between the corporate control debate and fundamental theories of social structure. Inspired by the excitement of these new ideas, I began working on the "Mathematical Analysis of Corporate Networks" project directed by Professor Schwartz. My dissertation, and this book, evolved from my work on this project.

I am grateful to the many people who have assisted me at various points in this research. My greatest debt is to Michael Schwartz, who initiated the project of which this study is a part. His dynamism and enthusiasm helped make this research a truly exciting enterprise. It is a privilege to have been associated with him. David Bunting made his data available to me, as well as his copious knowledge of American economic and business history. Without his generosity and assistance, this book would not have been written. G. William Domhoff provided encouragement and advice which contributed significantly to the completion of the book. It is hardly necessary to mention the tremendous debt that all researchers in this area owe to him. Mark Granovetter was a constant source of intellectual and moral support. His suggestions were invaluable during every stage of the study. Eugene Weinstein offered a wide range of theoretical and methodological pointers.

Special thanks are due to the following people who have read and commented on various parts of the manuscript: Howard Aldrich, Charles Hoffmann, Peter Mariolis, Beth Mintz, Ephraim Mizruchi, Donald Palmer, and Charles Perrow. William G. Roy provided a particularly detailed set of constructive criticisms. Thanks also to Edward Royce and Yinon Cohen.

Parts of this research were indirectly funded by the National Science Foundation, Grant SOC73-05606. William Atwood provided many hours of computer assistance.

Finally, I want to acknowledge the assistance and support of my wife, Katherine. The book is dedicated to her.

Mark S. Mizruchi
New Rochelle, New York

CHAPTER 1

THEORIES OF
THE MODERN CORPORATION

The large corporation is a basic institution in contemporary American society, hailed by some as a bastion of technological and managerial efficiency, and feared by others as a danger to individual freedom. But although the corporation is both praised and vilified, very little is actually known about it. This statement may appear peculiar considering the copious amount of theorizing by social scientists in recent years. However, an examination of the major works by sociologists, economists, lawyers, and business scholars yields the finding that, despite the sophistication of many theoretical arguments, there is very little evidence either in support of or in opposition to the major perspectives. The observation of one prominent scholar twenty years ago that "oddly, the so-called 'capitalist system' knows relatively little about itself" (Berle, 1959a: xiii) is to a great extent true today.

Despite this paucity of knowledge, certain developments have been accepted by most observers of the corporate scene. Many of these fall under the heading of what has been called "managerialism." This view, although forcefully challenged in recent years, remains the basis for much of contemporary social theory. Stated briefly, managerialism is the idea that large corporations have become powerful, autonomous institutions, largely independent of external influence or control. As large bureaucracies, they are increasingly able to shape and control their environments, rather than being controlled by them. In addition, the phenomenon of corporate "interest groups," or several companies under a common center of influence, has essentially disappeared, as insiders have gained control of their particular corporations. Thus, fundamental conflicts of interest abound in the corporate world, and the idea of a unified business elite has passed into the realm of modern folklore.

This study is an examination of the structure of relations among large corporations in the twentieth-century United States. The aim is to contribute to an assessment of the managerialist argument and to offer an alternative perspective on the debate over corporate control. While a number of studies have assessed the managerialist position in recent years, few have looked at the problem from a historical perspective. Although the managerialist argument explicitly rests on a number of assumptions about the development of the American corporate structure in the twentieth century, studies of this development have almost invariably focused on a single point in time. Those which have viewed the issue as one of historical development have generally limited themselves to comparisons of two different years, typically one from the 1930s and one from the 1950s or 1960s (Perlo, 1957; Dooley, 1969; Allen, 1978). The present study begins at the turn of the century, and analyzes the American corporate system into the mid 1970s.[1] In so doing, it provides a considerable amount of data to an area noted for an absence of meaningful information.

For many years, social scientists thought it unnecessary to provide detailed evidence in support of the managerialist position. Indeed, in 1967, one of the pioneers in the field wrote that "the fact of the corporate revolution is now so widely accepted that statistical evidence is no longer needed to establish its occurrence" (Means, 1968: xxix). But evidence from recent studies has rendered this claim premature at best. If anything, to quote Sorokin in another context, "individuals have been speculating too much and studying the facts too little." Perhaps "it is . . . time to abandon speculation for the somewhat saner method of collecting the facts and studying them patiently" (Sorokin, 1927; quoted in Blau and Duncan, 1967: 2). At our present state of knowledge, this appears to be good advice.

*Causes and Consequences
of the Managerial Revolution*

Managerialism is not a single, monolithic concept, but rather a general view of corporations which has been put forth by a number of prominent theorists. The classic statement of this position was provided by Berle and Means (1968). The authors argued that a set of changes occurred in the United States in the early 1900s which altered the relations between private property and corporate control. As corporations became ever larger, the wealthy families who owned most of the firms' stock became less and less able to maintain their majority holdings. Thus, "a new market for corporate securities was sought in the man of smaller income, the employee, and the local customer" (Berle and Means, 1968: 58-59). As a consequence, the stockholdings were dispersed. A growing number of companies had no individual or family able to muster the majority of shares necessary for control. As this situation became more common, control gradually passed from stockholders to the insiders, those who ran the daily operations of the firm. Hence, ownership was separated from control.

Several consequences followed from this presumed trend. Since insiders now controlled the corporation, the argument goes, they were freed from the necessity of placating the stockholders. Stockholders, widely dispersed and removed from actual corporate operations, were lulled into a state of complacent passivity, content to receive their dividends, but unwilling and unable to confront management over policy. Managers were now free to pursue other aims. Dividend payouts were lowered, increasing the amount of capital available for reinvestment, thus freeing corporations from dependence on banks and other financial institutions. No longer subject to the dictates of profit maximization, corporate managers could concentrate on areas such as growth, sales, public relations, and even charitable and cultural concerns. This led at least one prominent theorist to proclaim the emergence of the "soulful corporation" (Kaysen, 1957).

Corresponding with the above trends was a decline in the existence of intercorporate control groups. Early in the twentieth century, individuals such as J. P. Morgan, John D. Rockefeller, and Edward H. Harriman simultaneously controlled several corporations apiece. It was thus possible to speak of corporate "interest groups," corporations under a common source of control, or with a basic unity of interest. According to the managerialist position, as stock dispersal proceeded and corporate control passed to insiders, the commonality of interest among large groups of corporations declined. The economy increasingly consisted of "a plurality of partly agreed, partly competing, and partly simply different groups" (Dahrendorf, 1959: 47).

LARGER CONSEQUENCES

The changes attributed to managerialism pointed to consequences far beyond the boundaries of particular corporations, or even the economy as a whole. Some theorists suggested that the separation of ownership from control paved the way for the dissolution of the "capitalist class" or of capitalism altogether. Dahrendorf (1959), for example, argued that the rise of the joint stock company signaled the age of "post-capitalist" society. According to this view, as ownership and control were separated, effective control of capital passed to managers, who were legally employees of stockholders. Thus, those who owned did not control and those who controlled did not own. This situation, argued Dahrendorf, led to the "decomposition of capital." Since control was based on one's position within the bureaucratic hierarchy, corporations became indistinguishable from other large bureaucratic organizations.

A similar argument was presented by Bell (1960). Suggesting that the kinship system provided the basis for the control of capitalist enterprise, Bell (1960: 42) argued that the separation of ownership and control destroyed the system of private property in the means of production on which capitalism rested: "No longer are there America's 'Sixty Families.' . . . The chief consequence, politically, is the breakup of the ruling class."

According to Riesman (1953: 242), "the captain of industry no longer runs business" and hence "no longer runs politics." Instead, the American political system is characterized by an absence of any one controlling group, and is instead influenced by a continuously changing array of "veto groups." And Parsons and Smelser (1957: 254) argued that "the original 'captains of industry' . . . failed to achieve or to exercise sufficient cumulative advantages to consolidate control of the enterprises in their families and their class." This inability to consolidate control so that it could be passed on to succeeding generations was both a cause and consequence of the separation of ownership from control.

So as capitalists lost control of their corporations and companies became increasingly atomized with more specific interests, the idea of a unified corporate elite became less plausible. Meanwhile, the growing divisions within the elite were seen as the basis for the pluralistic, democratic political system in the United States (Schumpeter, 1942; Dahl, 1970; Rose, 1967; Riesman, 1953; Bell, 1960; Lipset and Schneider, 1973).

IMPLICATIONS FOR SOCIOLOGICAL THEORY

The managerialist position contained important implications for sociological theory. It had direct effects in three areas: organization theory, political sociology, and social stratification.

In research on organizations, the managerialist position manifested itself in two ways. First, the emphasis on control by bureaucratic managers rather than capitalists suggested a similarity between corporations and bureaucracies in general. This similarity has been most evident in the claim that corporations are no longer subject to profit maximization. In fact, a number of theories of the firm have posited several different managerial motives, of which profits are but one (Simon, 1957; Baumol, 1959; Cyert and March, 1963; Marris, 1964; Williamson, 1964; Galbraith, 1967). Second, the managerialist claim that corporations have become independent from financial institutions as well as from one another has encouraged a focus on the individual firm as the unit of analysis. Thus, rather than beginning with a system of several corporations and viewing particular firms within that context, organization theorists have typically begun with the individual firm, while treating the environment as a residual factor. In recent years, as interorganizational analysis has become more common, there have been more attempts to relate organizational behavior to larger societal processes (Perrow, 1979; Aldrich, 1979). Criticisms of conventional organization theory have led to a variety of new perspectives (Benson, 1977; see also Chapter 2, this volume). The viability of these alternative approaches hinges strongly on the accuracy of the managerialist thesis.

In political sociology, an entire generation of theorists and researchers drew on managerialist assumptions to conclude that American society was pluralistic in nature, governed not by a particular elite or class, but rather by various pressure groups drawn from a wide cross section of the population. Empirical research in the United States has typically focused on voting behavior, and the existence of pluralism has been implicitly or explicitly assumed (Seybold, 1978). When pluralism was questioned by Mills (1956), criticisms of Mills typically referred to the separation of ownership from control as evidence that his conclusions about the relation between property and power were unwarranted (for example, see Bell, 1960; Parsons, 1968; Rose, 1967; Dahl, 1970). As Arnold Rose, a prominent pluralist theorist, pointed out, if the corporate elite is not essentially united, it is impossible to argue that business controls the government. In recent years, alternatives to pluralism based on Millsian and Marxist perspectives have reemerged (Domhoff, 1980). These alternatives are based on a belief in the essential unity of the corporate elite. Thus, the extent of unity within the corporate system has major consequences for the field of political sociology.

Finally, in stratification research, the concept of class based on property relations has been either ignored or dismissed as irrelevant. Instead, criteria such as occupational prestige and education have been employed as indicators of class, and mobility between different occupational strata has become a principal concern of contemporary research (for a symposium on this topic, see the January 1980 issue of *Contemporary Sociology*). This trend, too, has roots in the managerialist position. An example is provided in this passage from a contemporary classic in American stratification research:

> Class may be defined in terms of economic resources and interests, and the primary determinant of these for the large majority of men is their occupational position. To be sure, Marx stressed that the criterion of class is not a man's occupation but whether he is an employer who has the capital to buy the labor of others or an employee who sells his labor. This criterion, however, is no longer adequate for differentiating, as Marx intended it to do, men in control of the large capitalistic enterprises from those subject to their control because *the controlling managers of the largest firms today are themselves employees of corporations* [Blau and Duncan, 1967: 6; emphasis added].

As in the other areas, these assumptions have recently been questioned by some researchers (Braverman, 1974; Wright and Perrone, 1977; Moore, 1980; Horan, 1978; Beck et al., 1981). However, this questioning is a relatively new development. Most contemporary stratification research continues to focus on occupational mobility and status attainment.

SUMMARY

The issue of corporate ownership and control has far-reaching implications for sociological theory. If the managerialist position were incorrect, a new orientation to organizations, political sociology, and stratification might be necessary. Corporate organizations might have to be distinguished from nonprofit bureaucracies; the pluralist position in political sociology would receive a serious blow; and stratification research would be forced to seriously consider class as a function of property relations. Given the salience of these issues, the empirical accuracy of the managerialist thesis becomes an issue of crucial importance. We now turn to an examination of the evidence.

The Evidence for Managerialism

Since the original Berle and Means study (1968), a number of studies have addressed the issue of corporate ownership and control. In recent years, two exhaustive reviews of these studies have appeared (Zeitlin, 1974; Mintz, 1978). Hence, the present review will be brief, and will focus on sifting through general issues and findings, rather than providing an in-depth review of each study.

Berle and Means analyzed the 200 largest nonfinancial corporations in the United States in 1929. Defining "management control" as a situation in which the largest stockholder owned less than 20 percent of a corporation's stock, they found that 44 percent of these 200 corporations could be classified as "management controlled." This study was replicated 30 years later by Larner (1970), who lowered the criteria for management control to less than 10 percent. Despite Larner's stricter criteria, he found that 84 percent of the 200 largest nonfinancial corporations in the United States (in 1964) had no individual stockholding of 10 percent or more. These results, when compared with those of Berle and Means, suggested that the corporate revolution which supposedly began early in the twentieth century was now close to complete.

Persuasive as this evidence was, these studies have been challenged on several grounds. First, a thorough examination of Berle and Means reveals that their conclusions far exceeded their data. As Zeitlin (1974) has demonstrated, only 22 percent of Berle and Means's 200 corporations could be definitely classified as management controlled. Of the 106 industrials in this group, only 3.8 percent were clearly management controlled. For the remaining 22 percent of management controlled firms, Berle and Means in fact had no information, and simply classified them as "presumably" management controlled. Second, a study conducted by the Temporary National Economic Committee (TNEC, 1940) uncovered the locus of control in 15 of Berle and Means's management controlled firms. Now if

Larner's results are accurate, then the findings of fewer management controlled firms in the Berle and Means data would only increase the magnitude of the managerial revolution. But Larner's results have been disputed by a number of recent studies, including those by Villarejo (1961), who found identifiable ownership control in 54 percent of the largest 250 U.S. industrials from 1960, and Sheehan (1967), who, using Larner's approach for 1967 data, found owner control in 29 percent of the largest 500 nonfinancial corporations, compared with Larner's 19 percent for the same sample.

Perhaps of even greater significance were two studies which took different approaches, those of Burch (1972) and Kotz (1978). Rather than employing the Securities and Exchange Commission's (SEC's) official stock ownership data, as Larner had done, Burch (1972) conducted an exhaustive search through business periodicals for information on the control of 500 large industrial corporations from 1950 to 1971. A corporation was categorized as "probably family controlled" if 4 percent to 5 percent of its stock was owned by a single interest and the family was represented on the firm's board. Using these criteria, Burch found that 60 percent of the 300 largest companies in the study were either probably or possibly family controlled. This result is markedly different from Larner's, in which at most 19 percent were family controlled. The reports of family stockholdings in the business press were also considerably different from those in the SEC reports; in nearly all cases, figures in the business press were higher, and Burch argues persuasively that the latter data are more reliable.

The study by Kotz (1978) focused on a subject which has become increasingly significant since World War II: institutional investors. In the mid 1960s, the House Committee on Banking and Currency, chaired by Wright Patman, gained authority to gather previously unavailable information on the stockholdings of bank trust departments (Patman Committee, 1968). The data showed that in 147 of the largest 500 industrial corporations in the United States, a particular bank held 5 percent or more common (voting) stock. Included among these were 36 corporations which had been classified by Larner as management controlled. Employing these data, as well as data from subsequent government investigations, Kotz studied the 200 largest U.S. nonfinancial corporations from the period 1967-1969. Basing his criteria primarily on a 5 percent level of stockholding (following a suggestion by the Patman Committee), Kotz found that as many as 40 percent of these corporations could be considered "bank controlled."

Family or Financial Control?

The idea of bank control introduced a new dimension into the debate. Previously, the question revolved around whether firms were management or family controlled. Berle and Means had employed the concept of "control through a legal device," a situation in which a holding company owned controlling stock in another company, which in turn controlled a third company, and so on. However, although 20 percent of the firms in Berle and Means's study were placed in this category, subsequent studies tended to ignore it. In a sense this was curious, given the considerable emphasis on the power of investment banks earlier in the century (for example, see Brandeis, 1914; Youngman, 1907; Moody, 1919; Carosso, 1970; Corey, 1930; Allen, 1935). On the other hand, the belief in the declining power of banks was so pervasive among American social scientists in the 1930-1970 period that the absence of discussions of bank control may not have been surprising.[2]

In fact, the issue of bank control and the distinctions between family and financial control of industry have posed serious conceptual problems for critics of the managerialist thesis. While Lundberg (1937), Villarejo (1961), Burch (1972), and Zeitlin (1974) have emphasized family control of corporations, Lenin (1975), Perlo (1957), Fitch and Oppenheimer (1970), and Kotz (1978) have focused on bank control. Others, such as Rochester (1936), Menshikov (1969), and Knowles (1973), have employed both concepts, sometimes interchangeably, and not always consistently.

The concept of bank control of industry appeared early in the twentieth century in a study by Hilferding (1981). Many of these ideas were later popularized by Lenin (1975). According to this argument, as capitalism developed, the growing concentration of the banking system created a tremendous amount of power in large banks. In the expansionary trend which characterized capitalist societies around the turn of the century, only the largest financial institutions possessed the capital necessary for large-scale investment. The banks were thus able to determine how and where capital would be employed. An examination of American economic history leaves little doubt that banks were extremely powerful during this period (see Chapter 2). But, as we have seen, a major element of the managerialist view is that corporations gradually gained independence from banks through their ability to finance investment with internally generated funds. Thus, as family control declined, so did bank control. And yet a closer examination reveals that the two types of control are very much logically independent of one another. A corporation can be family controlled but not bank controlled, if the corporation is able to achieve its goals without submitting to bank influence. But a corporation can also be bank controlled even if internally it is management controlled. In this case, its dependence on the bank exists regardless of whether the firm is family or management controlled. Furthermore, and this is a condition rarely discussed by researchers in this area, a corporation can be controlled by a family and simultaneously controlled by a bank. For example, although Zeitlin (1974) provides considerable evidence to suggest that Kennecott Copper has historically been controlled by the Guggenheim family, the National Resources Committee provided a convincing argument that the firm was controlled by J. P. Morgan & Co. (Sweezy, 1953). The point is that both positions may be correct at the same time. As an individual corporation, Kennecott may have been family controlled; but this does not prohibit the possibility that, from an interorganizational perspective, the company was bank controlled.

The difficulty with both the Burch (1972) and the Kotz (1978) studies, as well as the others discussed, is that their classifications of control are based on the legal characteristics of individual firms. However, control relationships are ultimately social relationships, and individual corporations always exist in an environment populated by other corporations with which they must interact.[3]

Since Berle and Means, all studies of stock dispersal have assumed that a particular interest can control a corporation with a minority stockholding. Hence, in these cases, the stock alone cannot be the basis for control. John D. Rockefeller, Jr., was able to control Standard Oil of Indiana despite the fact that he owned only 14.9 percent of its stock (Berle and Means, 1968), and, in more recent years, corporations can be controlled with as little as 5 percent or less (Kotz, 1978). At the same time, in some cases even total stock ownership cannot assure control over a corporation. Thus, in 1962, as a sanction for previous behavior, a group of 17 banks and insurance companies placed Howard Hughes's 78 percent interest in TWA aside in a trust fund while they administered the firm (Fitch and Oppenheimer, 1970). In this case, even Hughes's nearly total stock ownership was insufficient for control. In addition, it has been suggested that historically, powerful bankers actually preferred the wide dispersal of stock because it enabled a corporation to be more easily controlled. Writing about the power of J. P. Morgan early in the twentieth century, Corey (1930: 284) pointed out that:

> the House of Morgan and other financial masters of industry did not own the corporations under their control. Nor was ownership necessary. Stockholders being scattered and numerous (43,000 in the case of United States Steel) control was easily usurped by minority interests, particularly when these interests were *institutionalized* in the formidable combination of the House of Morgan [emphasis added].

Hence, it was not the legal criterion of stock ownership which determined who controlled a corporation. Rather, control involved a complex set of institutional relationships, and it was control over this system of relationships which determined the ultimate control over a particular corporation.

> The Morganization of industry was accomplished by a complex system of stock ownership, voting trusts, financial pressure, interlocking of financial institutions and industrial corporations by means of interlocking directorates, the community of control of minority interests—all dependent upon stockholders who did not participate in management, who could not easily combine to assert their ownership, and whose concern was limited to dividends [Corey, 1930: 284].

Thus, the separation of ownership and control in the sense described by Berle and Means may have been precisely what was necessary for financiers such as J. P. Morgan to exert control over corporations.

In a sense, then, this view of corporate power appears quite similar to that espoused by managerialists. It was Berle and Means who spoke of institutional position as more significant for corporate control than legal ownership of property, as the title of a later book by Berle (1959b; *Power Without Property*) indicates. Nevertheless, there is a crucial distinction between the two based on the unit of analysis. For Berle and Means (and others), the unit of analysis was the individual corporation. The prevalent types of corporate control in the economy were determined by aggregating the characteristics of individual firms. In the view advanced here, the corporation must be viewed as an element of an interorganizational system, in which no one corporation can be understood without locating its position within the system. Interestingly, this view flows straight from the analysis of Berle and Means themselves.

Berle and Means (1968: 66) originally defined a firm's management as its board of directors. Corporate control was defined as "the power to select the board of directors." Formally, of course, it is the stockholders who select the board. However, Berle and Means argued, as the stockholders were gradually dispersed, the board became a self-perpetuating oligarchy. The

significance of this argument for our purposes lies in its definition of "management." Later proponents of managerialism took
Berle and Means to mean the officers rather than the board of
directors (Burnham, 1941; Galbraith, 1967; Bell, 1973;
Chandler, 1977). The board was increasingly viewed as a passive
rubber stamp of management, as more or less "window dress-
ing" (Mace, 1971). Taking this argument a step further,
Burnham, Galbraith, Bell, and others argued that as technology
became more complex, real power became lodged in the scientists, engineers, and technicians, those whom Galbraith (1967)
termed the "technostructure." Yet despite these "knowledge is
power" arguments, the original Berle and Means position provided the possibility for a very different interpretation of
corporate control, one which the authors themselves never
followed up on. For if directors controlled corporations, then
by careful placement of a company's directors on the board of
another, the possibility for control through director representation existed. If institutional position conferred power upon the
board, then a corporation with strategically placed representatives on the boards of other corporations could exert control, or
at least influence, over those firms.

Thus, the concept of interlocking directorates as a mechanism of corporate control, so often discussed in the early part
of the twentieth century, flowed directly from Berle and
Means's original analysis. Interestingly, in their later works both
authors seem to have ignored this point, and instead embraced
the definitions of control put forth by latter-day managerialists.
But the issue is far from resolved, as we shall see in the
following section.

Discussion

The previous discussion raises three main points: First, control is a social phenomenon, not a legal one. Studies based on
stock ownership may fail to locate effective control of a corporation because stockholdings, large or small, may not in fact
serve as a basis for control. Second, family control and financial

control are analytically distinct categories, which may or may not coincide. While family control may operate at the level of the individual firm or at the level of intercorporate relations, financial control always operates at the level of intercorporate relations. Thus, a firm can be under financial control at the interorganizational level regardless of whether it is under family or management control at the organizational level. Because financial control always operates at the interorganizational level, it would appear necessary to begin any examination of corporate control at the interorganizational level of analysis.

Finally, in order to further proceed with this analysis, two additional questions must be confronted. First, if one argues that control over institutions is the source of power within a social system, this begs the question of what the source of this control is. Zeitlin (1974) and others agree that control over institutions is crucial, but they argue that the kinship system is the source of this control. In this line of reasoning, the kinship system and constitutions of particular families must be studied in order to understand a topic such as corporate control. The ascendence, for example, of David Rockefeller to the head of Chase Manhattan Bank would be seen as resulting from his family's control of the bank.

This view thus reasons that the family system is at the heart of the class system, and that the "capitalist class" must be understood as a group of closely interacting families. This argument is very persuasive because it provides an explanation for the origins of institutional control, and it is not necessarily inconsistent with the view advanced here. Its problem is that it ignores the possibility that a particular institutional structure can exist independent of the constitution of its membership, and that this can occur without in any way altering the basic character of the structure. Once an industrial enterprise is established, it may take on its own set of imperatives irrespective of who its controlling members are. As Zeitlin (1974) has pointed out, most of the evidence on the profit performance of owner versus management controlled firms indicates that they perform approximately equally. The reasons for this are fairly straightforward: Corporations are constrained by the markets within which they operate. They must attain certain levels of profitability and growth in order to survive. Similarly, banks must make choices based on their own market requirements. This situation suggests that capitalism may exist and operate under a basic set of systemic requirements regardless of the family backgrounds of the leaders of particular corporations. Financial institutions may be able to influence or control non-financial corporations regardless of the family backgrounds of their directors and officers.

One possible exception to this might be cases in which family-based interest groups induce "reciprocal" behavior between firms under their control. For example, back when the DuPont family controlled General Motors, they acquired U.S. Rubber, which, according to *Fortune*, sold tires to GM at slightly more than the cost of production. Since the DuPonts owned more stock in GM than in U.S. Rubber, their family fortune may have increased at the expense of the remainder of U.S. Rubber's stockholders (Fitch and Oppenheimer, 1970). But, even here, there is no reason to assume that this type of behavior could not occur within a purely financially based interest group. Fitch and Oppenheimer in fact give several examples of this type of situation, which appear to occur independently of the particular family interests involved.

The preceding argument again highlights a major problem with the managerialist view. As we have seen, the basis of the managerialist position was that the separation of ownership from control led to the growing independence and autonomy of corporate managements. However, there is no reason to assume that this separation had the consequences the managerialists attributed to it. Despite the importance of the studies by Burch, Kotz, Villarejo, and others, it is hard to deny that a consider-able amount of stock dispersal has occurred even since the Berle and Means study. But this separation of legal ownership from control does not in any way assure the independence of cor-porations from the market, from banks, or from one another. The profit performance of owner versus management controlled firms appears to be about equal. And the ability of corporations to finance investment from internally generated capital has failed to increase since Berle and Means's time (Lintner, 1959), and may have even decreased since 1955.[4] In summarizing the evidence on stock dispersal, Mintz (1978: 19) commented that "Berle and Means identified an important trend . . . and the studies which have followed their lead seem to agree that this trend has continued." However, she continued:

> The data . . . , interpreted in their best light, simply state that stock concentration is not of sufficient magnitude to produce control. These findings reveal nothing about the position of management nor the extent to which corporate power rests with the organization [Mintz, 1978: 19].

In addition, "they cannot address the possibility of another nucleus of control—financial institutions for example" (Mintz, 1978: 19).

In sum, the freeing of corporate managements from the influence of stockholders does not necessarily free them from the influence of other external forces such as banks. This final question must be thoroughly investigated at the empirical level.

NOTES

1. Although to my knowledge only two previous American studies have dealt with the period prior to the 1930s (Bunting and Barbour, 1971; Roy, 1977, 1981), a number of European studies have encompassed the entire twentieth century. For a review of this literature, see Fennema and Schijf (1979). A new study by Herman (1981) also deals with the early 1900s.

2. Even several leading Marxist thinkers accepted the belief in the declining power of banks (Sweezy, 1941; Baran and Sweezy, 1966). See Mintz (1978) for a review of this position.

3. Scott (1979) makes a similar point. See his excellent study, *Corporations, Classes, and Capitalism,* which treats many of the issues discussed here.

4. Fitch and Oppenheimer (1970: part 2, 73-74) cite a study by the Federal Reserve Board of San Francisco which demonstrates a sharp increase in reliance on external financing during the 1960s. See also Sweezy and Magdoff (1975).

CHAPTER 2

APPROACHES TO THE STUDY OF INTERLOCKING DIRECTORATES

This study is an attempt to bolster the empirical foundation for assessing the claims of managerialism. The approach will consist of a longitudinal study of the network of interlocking directorates among a sample of large American corporations. Three general characteristics of the structure will be examined. First, the relative connectivity of the network will be employed as an indicator of intercorporate cohesion and interdependence. Second, the centrality of particular corporations will be employed as an indicator of their significance within the system. Finally, an examination of cliques within the network will assess the extent to which specific interest groups have evolved over time.

The data for this study consist of officer and director interlocks among 167 large American corporations for the years 1904, 1912, 1919, 1935, 1964, 1969, and 1974 (1904 has only 166 firms). The corporations include 100 industrials, 25 transports, 10 insurance companies, 20 banks, and 12 investment banks, all but the last constituting the largest firms in their sectors, as ranked by "capitalization." Capitalization is defined as the book value of issued stock plus funded debt at par. Asset value was not used because most corporations did not publish reliable data in the early years. The data were collected by David Bunting, whose primary sources were the *Manual of Statistics* for 1904 and *Moody's, Standard and Poor's,* the *Banker's Directory and Collection Guide,* and the *New York Stock Exchange Directory* for the succeeding years (Bunting and Barbour, 1971).[1] Since Bunting's original data did not

33

identify officers of banks and insurance companies, and since they are essential to the analysis here, I located bank and insurance officerships for directors who interlocked. Volumes I-IV of *Who Was Who* and the *Dictionary of American Biography* were used to determine whether bank and insurance directors who interlocked were in fact officers of the financial corporations.

By the standards of most other interlock studies, this sample of 167 corporations is small. Most studies have used at least 250 firms (for example, Dooley, 1969; Allen, 1974, 1978) and others as many as 797, the number in Mariolis's 1969 set, which has been used by several researchers (Sonquist and Koenig, 1976; Pennings, 1980). The largest set of all, that used by Bearden et al. (1975) and Mintz (1978), includes 1131 firms. Nevertheless, the historical sweep of our data set compensates for its relatively small size. Comparative data for the largest 100 industrials show that they maintained an approximately equal share of manufacturing assets between 1896 and 1964 (between 35 percent and 46 percent; see Bunting and Barbour, 1971: 320). Thus, although some important corporations may be omitted in certain years, the data set does provide a generally stable basis for comparison.

The use of interlocking directorates as a data source requires some discussion, because of the tremendous amount of controversy about their precise meaning. In general, interlocks have been employed in three different ways. First, they have been used as indicators of corporate control (Pujo Committee, 1913; Brandeis, 1914; Rochester, 1936; Perlo, 1957; Menshikov, 1969; Fitch and Oppenheimer, 1970; Knowles, 1973). The view here is that an interlock with another firm is a means of controlling that firm. Companies with large numbers of interlocks are assumed to be more capable of control than those with few interlocks.

A second use of interlocks is as an indicator of intercorporate cohesion, or community of interest (Sweezy, 1953; Dooley, 1969; Allen, 1978). In this view, interlocks are viewed as signs of common interest between two or more companies. A number of government and legal investigations of interlocks have viewed them as mechanisms for reducing competition among leading firms in particular industries (Travers, 1968; Blumberg, 1975; Bunting, 1977).

Finally, a third and more recent view of interlocks involves viewing them in terms of the requirements of particular organizations (Thompson and McEwen, 1958; Vance, 1968; Pfeffer, 1972; Allen, 1974; Bunting, 1976a; Pfeffer and Salancik, 1978; Burt, 1979; Burt et al., 1980; Pennings, 1980). In this view, known as the "resource dependence" perspective, interlocks are seen as a strategy available to organizations for pacifying certain elements in their environments. By "coopting" a board member from another company, a firm increases its control over its environment. This view is particularly important because it is based on an essentially managerialist view of corporate control. According to these theorists, directors are chosen by management for various reasons, the most important of which are the prestige their presence offers the firm, their expertise in certain areas, and the belief that their firms will be able to provide opportunities for favorable business transactions.

Before assessing the relative merit of these three views, one additional view must be confronted. Some authors have argued, either implicitly or explicitly, that interlocks are essentially meaningless (Galbraith, 1967; Stigler, 1968; Mace, 1971). The primary basis for this view is the idea that boards of directors are no longer powerful but are merely figureheads employed by top management to lend prestige to the corporation. This argument appears to have been effectively undercut by the evidence of the resource dependence theorists cited above. By showing that interlocking correlates significantly with important performance variables, these theorists have demonstrated that even a managerialist-based view of corporations can benefit from an analysis of interlocks. Furthermore, as Kotz has pointed out (and others had pointed out earlier), there is a major difference between "managing" the daily operations of a firm and actually having the power to determine general policy. The former involves making detailed decisions within the broader limits set down by the latter. Drawing on March and Simon (1958), Perrow (1976: 2) has pointed out that "as long as one can control the premises that are used to make choices among alternatives, one can leave the choices themselves up to the subordinate." Examples of a board stepping in to monitor, coerce, and even oust management abound. For example, after Anaconda Copper's Chilean properties were nationalized without compensation by the Allende government in 1971, Anaconda's president and four other officers were removed from the board and replaced by five representatives of Chase Manhattan Bank (Zeitlin, 1974). More recently, prior to the ouster of Robert Abboud as President of First Chicago Corporation, *Business Week* (February 11, 1980: 33) reported that First Chicago's board members were becoming disenchanted with Abboud's performance: "'Bob . . . has a new set of problems that are his own creation,' says a former top bank officer. 'Those problems are a lot harder to explain to the board.' " After a series of clashes between Abboud and other top officials, one director commented that " 'the image this kind of incident gives the bank is not one that the board is very happy about.' "

In another example, *Fortune* (September 24, 1979: 92) reported that the recent replacement of David Foster as Chief Executive Officer of Colgate-Palmolive Co. "was caused by a series of long-running differences of opinion with key members of the Colgate board over his managerial style. So long as all went well, Foster was safe, but once troubles began to surface, he was vulnerable." As Foster himself later admitted, "I think I disturbed the board" (*Fortune,* September 24, 1979: 92). And finally, after announcing that company founder Willard F. Rockwell, Jr., would soon be replaced by Robert Anderson as chairman of Rockwell International, "the board changed a bylaw to stipulate that the CEO (Anderson) will henceforth report directly to the board and not to the chairman (Rockwell)." This was designed "to squelch any doubts that Anderson is the man the board wants to run the company" (*Business Week,* August 28, 1978: 30).[2] Examples such as these could be multiplied indefinitely, but the point remains the same. Management of day-to-day affairs does not in itself constitute control over the corporation.

The three approaches to analyzing interlocks have yielded different but by no means contradictory findings. Researchers in the resource dependence tradition have found that a company's interlocks are correlated with characteristics such as size, profitability, debt-equity ratios, growth, and dividend payout ratios (Dooley, 1969; Pfeffer, 1972; Allen, 1974; Bunting, 1976a; Pfeffer and Salancik, 1978; Burt, 1979; Pennings, 1980). Dooley, for example, found that nonfinancial interlocking with financials was a direct function of size and debt (r^2 = .251). Pfeffer found that a corporation's proportion of "inside" (management) directors was negatively correlated with its debt-equity ratio ($r = -.34$) and the extent to which it is subject to local and national regulation ($r = -.365$ and $r = -.32$, respectively). The proportion of financial representatives on nonfinancial boards was also positively related to the latters' debt-equity ratios ($r = .21$). Allen found significant relationships between nonfinancial interlocks with financials and capital intensity, growth, and debt-equity ratio. These figures ranged from a low of $r = .08$ in the case of nonindustrial growth to $r = -.277$ for nonindustrial capital intensity. Bunting hypothesized a curvilinear relationship between interlocking and profitability for industrials at seven points between 1905 and 1974 and found statistically significant results ranging from r^2 = .032 in 1935 to r^2 = .41 in 1964. In sum, these studies all indicate that interlocks are significantly related to certain measurable organizational and environmental factors.

The two other types of interlock studies have employed interlocks either as measures of influence and/or control or as indicators that a cohesive elite exists. Early studies of interlocks as control mechanisms were primarily descriptive in nature and assumed rather than demonstrated the control that interlocks supposedly represented (Pujo Committee, 1913; Brandeis, 1914; Rochester, 1936; Perlo, 1957; Fitch and Oppenheimer, 1970). Only occasionally did these studies employ independent criteria to bolster their assertions about interlocks, and in these cases the external data were not systematically employed. Only recently, as interlocks have been used to examine theories of corporate control, have more systematic hypotheses about interlocking been developed (Mariolis, 1975; Bearden et al., 1975; Sonquist and Koenig, 1976; Mintz, 1978). These studies have examined hypotheses designed to test the bank control and alternative models of corporate organization. The general finding has been that major New York banks are the most heavily interlocked and most central corporations in the network. However, the implications of these data for the bank control thesis have been debated. Mariolis (1975) found that, despite the high number of bank interlocks (a mean of 27.5 versus 10.5 for all corporations), type of firm accounted for only 5.2 percent of the variation in centrality, a figure he deemed too low to provide conclusive support for the bank control thesis. Mintz argued that since a majority of the most central corporations were banks, that only a bank control model was consistent with this pattern. Until we have additional evidence on the character of relations between banks and nonfinancials, such debates are likely to continue.

A third use of interlocks has been as a means of identifying individuals who constitute an "inner group" of the capitalist class (Zeitlin, 1974). Those who sit on several boards are compared with single or few-board members for involvement in civic, local, and national policy-making committees, and memberships in elite social clubs. Studies of this type on data for the United States have been conducted by Soref (1976), Koenig et al. (1979), Ratcliff et al. (1979), and Useem (1979). Perrucci and Pilisuk (1970) came to a similar conclusion based on interorganizational network memberships in a small city. In these studies a common finding is that, *ceteris paribus*, those who have multiple board positions are more likely than single-board directors to be members of other elite groups. Soref, for example, found that multiple-board directors were significantly more likely than single-board directors to have elite backgrounds, and be members of exclusive social clubs, a finding replicated by Koenig et al. Ratcliff et al. found that multiple-board directors were more likely to be involved in leadership positions in community organizations, including the United Way campaign and university boards of trustees. And Useem found that multiple-board directors were disproportionately represented in cultural, charitable, philanthropic, educational, governmental, economic advisory, and other kinds of organizations, as well as elite social clubs. These data strongly suggest that interlocking individuals are particularly important in other areas of society. However, their meaning for the particular corporations involved is less clear.

On the whole, then, these studies indicate that interlocking directorates are significant phenomena. They are positively correlated to a number of economic characteristics of particular corporations, and they are correlated with external activities of particularly important individuals. But whether they can resolve the corporate control debate is another matter. On the one hand, the available data indicate that a firm's network position as determined by interlocking has a positive effect on aspects such as growth, profitability, and debt. For example, while Bunting found that interlocks accounted for up to 40 percent of the variation in profit rates, type of control as determined by stock ownership has produced virtually no difference in profit rates (Larner, 1970; Kamerschen, 1968) or very small differences (Monsen et al., 1965; Palmer, 1973). On the other hand, the correlations derived by resource dependence theorists, although statistically significant, are generally somewhat low, usually in the .2 to .3 range. In light of this problem, the specific meanings of individual interlocks must be addressed. In the following sections I will discuss the extent to which interlocks can be viewed as mechanisms of coordination, cooptation, or control.

Interlocks as Coordination

Interlocks based on coordination have been the primary interest of legal and governmental analyses of collusion among members of a particular industry. These could also occur in cases of joint ventures between members of different industries (Pfeffer and Nowak, 1976) or in cases of "reciprocal" customer-supplier relationships (McCreary and Guzzardi, 1965). The first type, intraindustry interlocks, has been outlawed since the Clayton Antitrust Act of 1914. However, there is no law which prevents members of an industry from interlocking indirectly by sitting on the board of a third company, such as a bank. For example, in 1972, six of the eight largest U.S. oil companies interlocked indirectly through six major banks an average of 3.2 times with one another (Blair, 1976). However, in order to demonstrate that indirect interlocks are actually indicative of cooperative relations between competitors, the particular character of these interlocks must become known. If a bank sends different officers to each of two different oil companies, this will create an indirect interlock between the oil companies, but it is unlikely to constitute a mechanism by which the oil companies coordinate policy. However, if the two oil companies both sent officers to the bank board, then the former's direct representatives would sit together on the same board. Only these particular indirect interlocks are likely to constitute direct attempts by members of an industry to coordinate policy (this will be examined in Chapter 5).

Reciprocal relations between customers and suppliers are cases in which each firm provides the other with a particularly attractive and profitable deal, to the supposed benefit of both (McCreary and Guzzardi, 1965). For example, in the early 1960s, General Tire purchased construction equipment from Johns-Manville, which in turn purchased a film for the production of pressure-sensitive tape produced by General Tire. But while this process appears to involve cooperation and a principle of equal exchange, a closer examination of the available evidence suggests that in most cases a factor of coercion was involved. For example, when Stauffer Chemical, a customer of Anaconda, began building a new plant, the plan called for the use of an Anaconda competitor's mining machine cable. An Anaconda sales representative heard about this, and the next day the specifications were changed to accommodate Anaconda. Although there was no direct evidence in this particular case, most such cases involved participation by top officials of the companies. A tabulation of the McCreary and Guzzardi data indicates that, of the nine cases they discussed, seven involved some form of coercion of one company by another. In only two examples was it clear that both companies would benefit equally.

Fitch and Oppenheimer (1970) discuss several other examples of reciprocity, all of which appeared to involve coercion (as for example, the case in which U.S. Rubber sold tires to General Motors at cost). One particular example, taken from the 1965 Senate Antitrust Hearings, involved Jones and Laughlin Steel's purchase of tires from General Tire. Despite several protests from lower management that the tires were unsound, the purchase orders continued. The reason appeared to be that General Tire purchased enough steel from Jones and Laughlin to necessitate the reciprocal purchase. According to a survey conducted by *Purchasing* magazine, 78 percent of U.S. corporations with over $50 million in assets admitted to engaging in reciprocal activities of this nature (Fitch and Oppenheimer, 1970).

In sum, among the presumed "cooperative" intercorporate relationships, few are likely to involve a nonhierarchical, direct interlock between two companies. Intraindustry interlocks can be accomplished only by means of indirect links through third parties, and reciprocal relations between two companies appear more likely to contain elements of one-way coercion. It appears that most significant interlocks are best viewed in terms of either cooptation or influence. It is to these that we now turn.

Cooptation or Influence?

The view of interlocking directorates as mechanisms of cooptation has its theoretical roots in the work of Selznick (1949) and Thompson and McEwen (1958). Selznick, in his classic study of the Tennessee Valley Authority, found that the

TVA attempted to diffuse conflict by absorbing potentially disruptive groups into its formal structure. Selznick termed this tactic "cooptation." Thompson and McEwen later discussed several strategies with which organizations could cope with their environments, of which cooptation was one. According to Thompson and McEwen (1958: 27), "the acceptance on a corporation's board of directors of representatives of banks or other financial institutions is a time-honored custom among firms that have large financial obligations or that may in the future want access to financial resources." In subsequent studies, interlocks were viewed as mechanisms by which corporate managements coopted elements in their environments in order to reduce uncertainty.

Two points should be noted here. First, this view implicitly assumes management control of corporations. Corporate boards are assumed to be chosen primarily by the leading officers of the firm. Although managements are not considered independent of external influence (that is, as powerful) as in the original managerialist perspective, they are seen as the most powerful actors within organizations. Second, the cooptation model has an implicit view of the coopting organization as more powerful than the coopted organization. The ability to coopt a representative of another firm onto one's board is indicative of a corporation which is successful in dealing with its environment. However, a problem with this view is that it ignores the possibility that a corporation might actively attempt to influence another corporation by placing one of its representatives on the board of the other. As Aldrich (1979: 296) has observed, "the term cooptation may involve too much 'voluntarism' in some cases, such as when taking on a director from a bank is the price a firm pays for having its corporate bonds underwritten."

Let us consider another interpretation of the Thompson and McEwen example. Instead of the nonfinancial corporation coopting a bank by allowing a banker on its board (thus diffusing the conflict), perhaps the bank can expect a seat on the nonfinancial's board in order to monitor the latter's behavior. In this case, the bank is actively and aggressively pursuing its interests. The interlock is no longer viewed as cooptation, but is rather an example of *influence*. And, interestingly, there is nothing in this view which is inconsistent with the idea that possession of crucial resources enables a corporation to better cope with its environment. In fact, it is precisely the bank's control over a particular resource (in this case loan capital) which confers power upon it. Thus, interlocks can also be viewed as means by which one corporation attempts to exert influence over another. This might be termed a "modified" resource dependence model.[3]

However, two problems remain. First, as Burt (1979) and Palmer (1979) have pointed out, the process of discovering which interlocks are indicative of a particular attribute is extremely problematic. In a study of "broken ties," Palmer (1979) found that the majority of broken interlocks between companies were not renewed. In fact, among single-interlock ties, only 8 percent were renewed, while among multiple-interlock ties only 30 percent were renewed. This led Palmer to conclude that most interlocks are not indicative of actual intercorporate dependencies, although he concedes that "as many as three-quarters of all multiple-interlock ties are indicative of actual intercorporate relationships" (Palmer, 1979: 17). But even if we have reason to believe that an interlock is indicative of an important interorganizational connection, we still may have no information on exactly what function the interlock serves. If a broken interlock between a bank and an industrial is reinstated, is it a case of the industrial continuing to coopt the bank or of the bank continuing its influence over the industrial?

This dilemma is reminiscent of the debates over functionalism and conflict social theory or between pluralist and elitist models of the American political system. In both cases, general stalemates have existed for several years, and the best prospect for resolving the issues involves moving beyond the traditional approaches and concepts. In this study, I will present a synthesis of the cooptation and influence views, which, although narrowing the general level of the debate over managerialism, may help us to move beyond the formulations currently involved in the debate. This will involve three stages. First, an empirical analysis of correlates of interlock relations will be undertaken to examine the extent to which interlocks correspond with stock ownership relations. Second, a theoretical model of the meaning of interlocks and their role in the corporate control debate will be developed. And third, encompassing the major part of the study, a historical examination of the corporate network from the turn of the century to 1975 will be undertaken. A set of hypotheses related to the structure of the interlock network will be drawn from resource dependence literature or derived from the implications of managerialist works, and these will be examined using a variety of models developed for this purpose. By carefully analyzing the relation between the hypotheses and the findings, I hope to shed light on the character of intercorporate relations during the twentieth century.

Interlocks and Stockholding:
An Examination

The extensive data gathered by the Patman Committee (1968) provide us with an opportunity to examine the relation between interlocks and stock ownership information. These data have also been compiled by Kotz (1978), who attempted to determine the extent of bank control among 200 large American nonfinancial corporations. Using data from interlocks among 167 large American corporations in 1969 (described above), I made two comparisons. First, I took every case in which the Patman Committee classified a corporation as "bank controlled" on the basis of stock ownership of 5 percent or more and checked to see if a corresponding interlock existed. Second, I took all corporations classified by Kotz as under full or partial financial control and performed the same operation. For Kotz, the criteria for a corporation being classified as under full financial control included one of the following: (1) a 10 percent stockholding where no other stockholder had as large a block; (2) a 5 percent stockholding in which the bank was a leading supplier of capital or had "strong representation" on the nonfinancial's board of directors; or (3) "unique circumstances," in which other evidence suggested that there was clear financial control. The two data sets overlap considerably. The Patman data were based on 1967 information. Kotz's data were based partly on the Patman data and partly on the *Institutional Investor Study Report* issued by the Securities and Exchange Commission, based on data from 1969. Since my data are from 1969, the Kotz comparison is probably more accurate. Finally, since board representation is one criterion for Kotz's classification, leading to the possibility of a spurious relationship in the case of stock-interlock correspondence, I should point out that in only one case discussed here was board representation the basis for a bank control classification. In this particular case, Union Pacific (controlled by Brown Brothers, Harriman & Co.), Kotz's evidence appeared overwhelming.

The Patman report revealed 36 cases of a 5 percent or higher stockholding in a nonfinancial by a bank trust department in which the corporation was previously thought to be under management control. Of these, 26 were in my 1969 sample. Among the 26 cases of bank stockholding, only 12 involved an interlock between the 2 firms in question. Based on the density of the network as a whole (see Chapter 3), there was only a 4.6 percent chance at random that any 2 firms would interlock. Thus, the 46.2 percent chance of a large stockholding being accompanied by an interlock does indicate that stock ownership is strongly related to interlocking. However, it is far from an assurance that such a link will occur. Furthermore, only 5 of the 12 links involve bank representatives sitting on the boards of the nonfinancials. Hence, only 19.2 percent of the large bank stockholdings are accompanied by the presence of direct bank representation on the nonfinancial's board.

Comparisons based on the Kotz data reveal a similar pattern. Of the 45 corporations classified as under financial control for which we have data, only 20 (44.4 percent) involved interlocks between the firms in question. Financial representatives were involved in 14 of these 20 links, somewhat more often than in the Patman data, but still only 30.7 percent of the total number of connections.

Thus, while a large bank stockholding in a nonfinancial corporation is a strong predictor of interlocking between the two firms, it still is accompanied by interlocks less than half the time. When financial representation on the board of the non-financial is considered, these interlocks occur in fewer than one-third of the cases. Furthermore, in a number of cases, two or more financial institutions were involved, but only one or neither was interlocked. Thus, although Kotz classified United Aircraft under the domain of Chase Manhattan Bank (the firms have one interlock), United also exchanges officers with First National City Bank (Citibank) and interlocks with Morgan Guaranty Trust. NCR, which Kotz places under Morgan control, interlocks with Mellon National Bank and with Citibank, but not with Morgan. This, of course, does not demonstrate that interlocks in the absence of large stockholdings are *not* indicative of control relations. After all, as we have seen, stockholding has often been viewed as irrelevant to or unnecessary for control. However, the fact that large stockholdings do exist without interlocks necessitates a rethinking of the latter's precise role.

Interlocking Directorates and Influence:
A Network Perspective

The evidence discussed above, combined with that presented by Palmer, calls into question the extent to which an individual interlock can be indicative of a dyadic control relationship. In 1904, when J. P. Morgan & Co. placed three of its representatives on the board of U.S. Steel, it was a clear reflection of Morgan domination. But any given interlock may be no such indication.

However, there is an alternative way of looking at interlocks, derived from an orientation developed in small group research in the area of sociometry, which has recently been extended to the field of interorganizational relations. The basis of this view is that the relations among units in the social world can be

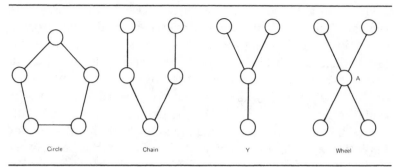

Circle   Chain   Y   Wheel

Figure 2.1   Four Types of Network Structure

mapped into a structure, and that this structure can provide insight into the character of the relations (Homans, 1950; Moreno, 1953; Mitchell, 1969; White et al., 1976). An early attempt to apply what is now called "network analysis" was made by William F. Whyte in his classic study, *Street Corner Society* (1943). By charting the friendship relations and lines of influence among members of the group he studied, Whyte was able to demonstrate that the character of group activities corresponded very closely with the form of the sociogram of relations. Doc, the gang leader, was the only person with close friendship ties to all three subgroups within the gang. Doc's leadership appeared to be a function of his centrality in the friendship network.

In subsequent studies, the concept of centrality was seen as a crucial variable in group activities. The definition of centrality typically employed was the one developed by Bavelas (1950). According to Bavelas, the most central point in a network was that which could reach the largest number of other points in the smallest number of steps. In a well-known study, Leavitt (1951) found that centrality in communication networks was strongly correlated with variables such as satisfaction in group activity, leadership, and influence on the outcome of events. By creating several different types of communication structures, Leavitt found that the perceived influence of the most central member was a function of the particular type of structure. Using four types of structure, the circle, chain, Y, and wheel (see Figure

2.1), Leavitt found that the differences between the most central figure and the others increased with the growing hierarchy of each structure. Studies by Bass (1949), Strodtbeck (1954), and March (1956) provide similar evidence of the relation between centrality (as measured by time spent interacting or by acts initiated) and influence. In a summary of this evidence, as well as a study of his own, Hopkins (1964) concludes that centrality is a strong predictor of both influence and rank (leadership). In his own study, the correlation between centrality and influence was .82 (see also Thibaut and Kelley, 1959, for additional references).

The term "influence" may have different meanings, based on two different ways of looking at centrality and group behavior. One type of focus is on the unified group working toward a common goal. In this situation, the topic of most of the studies cited above, the concept of centrality appears not only as an attribute of individuals but also as one of the group as a whole (MacKenzie, 1966; Nieminen, 1973). Thus an entire network is either highly centralized as in the wheel, or decentralized, as in the circle. The definition of influence in these studies is generally based on the ability to contribute to the completion of group tasks, rather than in terms of the ability to exercise power over other group members. Hopkins (1964: 3), for example, defines influence as "the effect an action has on the members viewed collectively, in particular the effect it has on the content and relative salience of shared norms." However, there is nothing in this view which is inconsistent with the idea that influence also involves coercion of some individuals by others. Even if influence is defined as the effect one has on defining and maintaining group norms, the maintenance of group norms itself may involve coercion.

What seems clear is that, to the extent that any group has a particular set of goals, the most influential member of the group will be the one best able to articulate and define those goals, whether or not it involves the coercion of other members. The available data on human interaction suggest that those in central positions within interpersonal networks appear most likely to influence the group as a whole.

But can this principle be applied to interorganizational networks as well? First of all, the types of links are usually defined differently in the two types of studies. Whereas small group research tends to focus on friendship patterns or on behavior in task-oriented experimental situations, interorganizational network analysis frequently focuses on formal group membership overlaps. This is both a blessing and a curse. On the one hand, it provides a purely objective view of network ties. On the other hand, membership overlap information is static and is not often accompanied by clear examples of interorganizational behavior. Thus, the content of interaction must either be inferred from the structure or from difficult to assemble and often unreliable behavioral data. Still, interorganizational network research has yielded data which can be compared with structural variables such as centrality. And indeed, one of the most frequent findings in interorganizational research is the consistently high correlation between centrality and reputed influence.

In the past decade, a number of studies have found a considerable correspondence between network centrality and influence. The first of these was conducted by Perrucci and Pilisuk (1970). Drawing on the work of Floyd Hunter (1953), Perrucci and Pilisuk studied a group of community leaders in a small midwestern city. The basis for comparison was the individual's number of leadership positions in various community organizations. The authors compared those with several positions, interorganizational leaders (IOLs), with single organizational leaders (OLs) and found that the IOLs were consistently seen by members of both groups as more influential on the outcomes of several community issues. As the authors conclude: "It is not the potency of the individual but the shape of the web (in which he is a node) which depicts the structure of enduring community power" (Perrucci and Pilisuk, 1970: 1044). These findings are also similar to those of the "inner group" theorists cited above.

While Perrucci and Pilisuk appear to be more concerned with the power of particular individuals than with the organizations they represent, it requires only a small step to speak of organizational power in this context. Organizations with heavily interlocked individuals are themselves likely to be heavily interlocked.

> Given the assumption that several organizations must combine resources to shape community decisions, power resources must also reside in the interconnections among organizations.... Thus the community banker who also sits on the executive boards of three other community organizations will occupy a more powerful situation than the banker who does not hold other executive positions [Perruci and Pilisuk, 1970: 1044].

This would suggest that, as an organization, the former executive's bank would be more powerful than that of the latter.

Two studies which took a somewhat different approach were those by Laumann and Pappi (1976) and Galaskiewicz (1979). These studies, based on community elite structures in small cities in Germany and the midwestern United States, divided community influence systems into separate structures based on particular resources. Using smallest space analysis, the authors presented graphic descriptions of community "influence structures." Laumann and Pappi (1976) were concerned with three such structures, those of "business-professional," "community affairs," and "social relations." They found that centrality in the economic and political structures was a fairly strong predictor of reputed influence in the community affairs and business-professional structures (r = .40 and .30, respectively), although the relation was less strong in the social relations network (r = .17).

Galaskiewicz (1979), employing a straightforward resource dependence view, hypothesized that the centrality of particular organizations within a network would correspond to its control over crucial resources. Basing the extent of interorganizational ties on replies to questions about an organization's dependence on other organizations, he found that financial institutions were the most central in the "money network," with industries in the second most central area. But the strongest indicator of an organization's effect on the outcomes of community issues was "the set of resources that actors [could] mobilize through their existing set of social relationships" (Galaskiewicz, 1979: 151). Hence, as with Perrucci and Pilisuk's study, the crucial variable in community influence was the character of one's interorganizational linkages. The correlations between perceived organizational influence and interorganizational resources (outflows) were .53, .51, and .55 for the three networks analyzed in the study.

Finally, a study by Rogers and Maas (1979) employed interviews with the top officers of 150 governmental and private agencies to determine correlates of organizational power. Power was viewed as composed of four attributes: possession of resources, control, influence, and obligation. Network centrality was considered indicative of control. In discussing how control of resources is converted into power, Rogers and Maas (1979: 7)

> submit that part of this process is achieved through the movement of organizations into positions of dominance in a network of organizations. . . . A critical element in this process is control of information and contacts with other units. . . . Actors located in the center of a network tend to play integrative roles, and come to possess power because . . . other parties must use the more central organization as a connecting link.

Rogers and Maas determined centrality in two ways: first, by whether officers of different organizations met to discuss interorganizational issues; second, in terms of joint activities undertaken by the two organizations. The first indicator was the strongest of ten predictors of an organization's reputed influence (r = .32). The second measure of centrality was the fourth largest predictor (r = .14). Another interesting finding was that leaders' appraisals of the power of their own organizations (termed "perceived" influence as opposed to "reputed" influence) had very little relation to influence reputed to their organizations by others (r = .12, not statistically significant). Furthermore, perceived influence had essentially no relation to either type of centrality (r = .03, r = − .04, neither statistically significant). This finding may not be entirely surprising. After all, even J. P. Morgan once denied under oath that he had any power (Allen, 1935). But it is a fact which, as we shall see, is well worth keeping in mind.

In sum, the evidence from both small group and interorganizational research leaves little doubt that influence as the potential for control is strongly related to network centrality. We can now apply this principle to the network of interlocking directorates. Let us consider a system of corporations in which information and resources are exchanged through connections among different firms. In this situation, the most centrally located corporations should be those that control the most crucial resources within the system. Since centrality appears to be a correlate of influence, then the corporations most central in the network should be most able to affect the outcome of interorganizational activities.

This perspective forces us to move beyond questions of the control inherent in specific dyadic relationships toward a concept of a structure, in which the role of a given link can only be understood in terms of its relation to the system as a whole. Instead of concentrating on which companies control specific other companies, we now focus on which companies are in positions to exercise the greatest amount of influence in situations of collective action.[4]

NOTES

1. Professor Bunting's assistance and generosity in making the data available to me is gratefully acknowledged.

2. Several cases from the early 1980s give further evidence of the dominant role of the board of directors: "The events that led to the ousting of Edgar H. Griffiths . . . and the appointment of Thornton F. Bradshaw . . . as RCA Corp.'s chairman and chief executive provide a rare view into the inner workings of a board when it is dissatisfied with its chairman's performance. . . . Almost since Griffiths took over as chief executive in 1976, the board sought long range plans . . . for each of RCA's operations. Instead it got an emphasis on short-term earnings. . . . In great part, the board's dissatisfaction with Griffiths stemmed from his management style as well as the way he dealt with the board. . . . He tended to pressure the board at the last minute into doing things his way,' says an insider. When the board balked,

Griffiths would lose his temper. 'He's a bully and a tyrant,' the source adds" (*Business Week*, February 9, 1981: 72-73). "Roy L. Ash, the chairman and chief executive of loss-plagued AM International for four years, has resigned those posts following a clash with directors over sources of critically needed new capital" (*New York Times*, February 24, 1981: D1, D21). His resignation was forced on by a "secret coup launched by an outside director . . . , John P. Birkelund, [who sought] to rebuild AM's shaky capital structure. . . . Short-term debt soared to $148 million by Oct. 31, up from $69 million the year before, and this caused concern on the board. 'The debt was getting dangerous,' says George Kelm, an AM International director" (*Business Week*, March 9, 1981: 32-33). At Toro Co. of Minneapolis, chairman David T. McLaughlin is "apparently not looking for a merger partner. He insists that the board wants the company to stay independent" (*Business Week*, March 9, 1981: 30). And at Munsingwear, Inc., the board had named A. Byron "Tubby" Reed chairman in October 1979. According to *Business Week*, "Under his leadership, the company [was] far from avant-garde. 'Finally, the board just lost patience,' explains one director. Last fall it selected Raymond F. Good . . . as Reed's successor as President and in January named him chief executive officer" (*Business Week*, May 12, 1980: 100-102). See also Bauer (1981).

3. This view is consistent with Zald's (1969: 102) suggestion that "control of external resources serves as a lever for board power when the organization finds it difficult to secure these facilities from other sources and requires this resource." Just as access to crucial resources gives power to outside directors within an organization, it also gives power to the organizations they represent.

4. An important analogy can be made here by incorporating Simmel's (1950) discussion of dyads and triads. According to Simmel, the moment a third person is introduced into a dyadic relation, the character of the original relation changes. The same insight can be applied to intercorporate ties. The presence of additional corporations in the network has important consequences for particular dyadic relationships, suggesting that no dyadic tie can be understood apart from its role in the network as a whole. For example, a case of a bank placing two representatives on the board of a nonfinancial corporation may not be indicative of a direct control relationship if the same firm has a similar interlock with a different bank. This may be one reason that individual interlocks have relatively low correlations with external variables. It is quite possible that these correlations would be stronger were centrality rather than interlocks employed as a variable.

CHAPTER 3

MEASUREMENT OF
NETWORK CHARACTERISTICS

Studies of interlocking directorates go as far back as the Congressional Investigation of 1913. That study, known as the Pujo Report, used interlock and other data to demonstrate the existence of a "Money Trust" dominated by a few New York financial institutions. Over the years, interlocks have been employed in studies by the National Resources Committee (see Sweezy, 1953), the Temporary National Economic Committee (1940), the Federal Trade Commission (1951), and more recently by social scientists, as well as by Congress (see Chapter 2). Most of these studies have employed frequency distributions of interlocks. That is, a company with 25 interlocks is considered more significant than one with only 10 interlocks. Even as studies using interlocks have become increasingly sophisticated both theoretically and methodologically, the interlocks themselves have been treated without qualitative distinctions.

For example, Dooley (1969), Allen (1974), Bunting (1976a), Pfeffer and Salancik (1978), Burt (1979), and Pennings (1980) concern themselves with relations between interlocking and variables such as size, profitability, debt-equity ratio, customer-supplier relationships, and stock ownership. In all cases, sophisticated statistical techniques are employed, ranging from multiple and curvilinear regression to differential equation models.

However, despite the sophistication of these studies, there are problems with their use of interlocks. First, they ignore the fact that certain firms, merely by virtue of larger boards, have a greater propensity to interlock. Other things being equal, a firm

with twenty directors will have a greater ability to establish ties
than a firm with only ten directors. Second, treating all interlocks equally ignores the crucial matter of with whom the firm
is tied. An interlock with a highly interlocked firm allows one
to reach far more other firms than one with an obscure firm.

These two problems were first pointed to in an article by
Phillip Bonacich (1972a).[1] Based in part on the earlier work of
Hubbell (1965), Bonacich's (1972a, 1972b) argument is that a
point's centrality in a network should depend on three criteria:
(1) the number of links to other points; (2) the "intensity" of
the links; and (3) the centrality of those with which one is
linked. For organizations, the number of potential linkers in
each unit can be accounted for in the measure of association
(intensity). If R is a matrix of relationships (r) and C equals a
point's centrality, then for each point i

$$C_i = r_{i1}C_1 + r_{i2}C_2 + \ldots + r_{in}C_n$$

or

$$C_i = \sum_{\substack{i=1 \\ j \neq i}}^{N} r_{ij} * C_j$$

where N = number of organizations linked with i;
     r_{ij} = intensity of the particular link; and
     C_j = centrality of the organizations linked with i.

To find C_i we must compute a matrix of overlaps (R). There
are several possible measures of association which can be used
here (for a discussion of these, see Mariolis et al., 1979). In the
present study, I shall use the measure developed by Mariolis
(1975):

$$r_{ij} = b_{ij} / \sqrt{d_i d_j}$$

where b_{ij} = number of members in common and
d_i and d_j = number of potential interlockers from
              each organization.

This measure has three advantages: First, following Bonacich, it controls for the number of potential affiliations that a company might possess; for example, a company with 40 directors on its board has more opportunities to interlock than one with 8. Second, the square root of $d_i * d_j$ minimizes the effect of increasing board size so that the importance of each additional member decreases; for example, the difference between boards of 4 and 3 members is much greater than that between boards of 17 and 16 members. Finally, this figure is equivalent to a Pearson product-moment correlation statistic prior to subtracting out the means; hence, r_{ij} can be interpreted as a correlation coefficient.

Centrality scores are calculated as a system of simultaneous linear equations in the form $C = RC$ where C is an N x 1 vector of centrality scores and R an N x N correlation matrix containing the measures of overlap r_{ij} (N = the number of points in the system). This equation as it stands has no solution. However, Bonacich (1972b) has demonstrated that by multiplying C by the largest eigenvalue (λ) so that $\lambda C = RC$, an approximation can be reached. Hence, in actuality,

$$C_i = \frac{1}{\lambda} \sum_{\substack{i=1 \\ j \neq i}}^{N} r_{ij} * C_j$$

where λ = the eigenvalue of the first principal component.

The calculation is identical to factor analysis. The first eigenvector will have all nonnegative or nonpositive values and there will be as many all-same-sign eigenvectors as there are discrete components in the graph. All other eigenvectors will have some negative and some positive values. Because the calculation produces one more unknown than the number of equations, the actual value of the centrality scores is arbitrary. The one arbitrary parameter is selected so that the firm with the highest centrality receives a score of 1.0. All other scores are then calculated on that basis so that scores range from 0 to 1.

Because the scores are calculated by simultaneous equations, we have a structure of relationships such that every element is in some way dependent on every other element. Any alteration of even one point will have repurcussions throughout the entire system. Thus, this approach is more relevant sociologically than one based on treating the individual corporations as the units of analysis, as the frequency distribution studies ultimately do. In our approach, the network, that is, the structure of relationships, is the unit of analysis.

Strength and Direction of Ties

The pure centrality measure still fails to distinguish between different types of interlocks. For example, in 1904, John F. Dryden, president and founder of Prudential Life Insurance, also sat on the boards of U.S. Steel and Equitable Trust. Assuming that Prudential was his principal affiliation, Dryden created ties for Prudential with both U.S. Steel and Equitable Trust. But, at the same time, he created a tie between Equitable and U.S. Steel. This tie, while created automatically from the other two, may in fact have been only an artifact of them. Recognizing this, Sweezy (1953) termed the first two types "primary" interlocks and the latter tie a "secondary" interlock. More recently, Bearden et al. (1975) and Mintz (1978) have employed Granovetter's concepts of strong and weak ties to describe this process. Using mainly small group research, Granovetter (1973) argued that qualitative distinctions may exist between different types of interpersonal ties. Of particular importance are the differences between intense friendship ties and looser acquaintance ties. Granovetter terms the former strong ties and the latter weak ties. Strong ties are more likely to be transitive (that is, if A is tied to both B and C, then B is likely to be tied to C), and more likely to exist within cliques. Weak ties, on the other hand, while not as intense, may be more important for rapid dissemination of information or for uniting various subgroups within a larger society. In fact, Granovetter suggests that the ability of a large group to unite may depend on the bridging function performed by weak ties.

This distinction will be employed in this study by accounting for the "principal affiliations" of interlocking directors. Principal affiliation is in most cases determined by whether a person is an officer of the firm in question. In a few cases, a director was considered principally affiliated with a particular corporation based on historical or biographical information. For example, in 1904 John D. Rockefeller was coded as principally affiliated with Standard Oil, even though he was no longer an officer of the firm. Strong ties are those directly involving one's principal affiliations.[2] In our Dryden example, the interlocks involving Prudential are treated as strong ties, while those resulting from the Prudential ties (such as the U.S. Steel-Equitable Trust link) are defined as weak ties. It should be pointed out that this incorporation of the concepts is not identical with Granovetter's definitions of the terms. The analogy used here is based on the idea that in this case the link between U.S. Steel and Equitable created by Dryden is not as intense, or significant, as the other two links he creates. Dryden's role in this weak tie may in fact approximate that of a person serving as a connection between two acquaintances.

This distinction is also important for our analysis of cliques. Specific cliques can exist and yet be difficult to detect because of weak ties. If we remove the weak ties from the network, we may be able to perceive distinct clusters which were invisible in the total network. For example, an analysis of 1962 data revealed one large cluster, yet five distinct groups appeared when the weak ties were removed (Bearden et al., 1975).

There is, however, a logical problem with this principle. Weak ties created by officer interlocks cannot serve as connectors between different cliques, since these ties specifically connect corporations which are strongly tied to the same firm. Only a purely neutral interlock, created by one who has no principal affiliation within the system (and hence creates no strong ties) can serve as a bridge between two otherwise independent subgroups. In a system in which all or most members had a principal affiliation, the removal of weak ties might make little difference for the identification of distinct subgroups in the manner discussed above. However, in the data set being used here, a consistently high percentage of directors have no officer-ship within the system. Much of this appears to be a result of the relatively small sample size, in which a number of individual directorships do not appear (for example, while George F. Baker was known to have held about 40 directorships in 1912, he held only 16 in our data set).

The weak tie distinction is important not only for its role in the identification of cliques, but also because by eliminating the "noise" created by incidental interlocks, it gives us a more accurate indicator of the centrality of various firms. Centrality is now based only on direct interlocks created by officers, and, as we have seen, these ties are likely to be qualitatively different from the weak ties.

Accounting for strong ties is still based on the assumption that the interlocks are symmetric. However, when Dryden sits on the board of U.S. Steel, it is likely that he serves as a representative of Prudential at U.S. Steel rather than vice versa. Hence, we can say that Prudential "sends" a director to U.S. Steel and that U.S. Steel "receives" a director from Prudential (Kotz, 1978, for example, equated a sending interlock with "board representation"). In line with the perspective discussed in the previous chapter, we would expect the sender to exercise a certain degree of influence over the receiver. Thus, the asymmetry in the directional relationship will be weighted in favor of the sending firm. This distinction is incorporated into the centrality index by means of a "weighted" measure of r_{ij} (Mintz, 1978).

Sending:

$$r_{ij} = \frac{W_s * S_{ij}}{\sqrt{d_i d_j}}$$

where S_{ij} = number of officers of firm i who sit on the board of firm j.

Receiving:

$$r_{ij} = \frac{W_r * T_{ij}}{\sqrt{d_i d_j}}$$

where T_{ij} = number of officers of firm j who sit on the board of firm i.

Exchange of officers:

$$r_{ij} = \frac{W_s \ * \ S_{ij} + W_r \ * \ T_{ij}}{\sqrt{d_i d_j}}$$

where W_s = weight of sender;

$\qquad W_r$ = weight of receiver; and

$W_s + W_r = 1.$

W_s and W_r have been set to .9 and .1, respectively. The assigned weights are, of course, arbitrary. As with most measures of this type, their value will ultimately be determined by the tenability of the results they produce.[3]

One final modification must be mentioned. In a small number of cases, two firms were so heavily interlocked with each other that their centrality scores became inflated, thus distorting the entire system. For example, in 1904, Equitable Life Assurance maintained 18 interlocks with its banking affiliate, Equitable Trust. This peculiarity gave both firms an exaggerated level of overall centrality. Because such situations are rare, yet have significant effects, I have followed Bearden et al. (1975) in limiting the number of recorded interlocks in r_{ij} to three.

ILLUSTRATION

Given the complexity of both the calculation of the centrality scores and the modifications discussed above, it would appear necessary to demonstrate that these concepts actually provide more relevant information than that provided by frequency distributions of interlocks. Mariolis, for example, found a correlation of .91 between number of interlocks and centrality scores using the Bonacich measure, and concluded that the two could be used virtually interchangeably. There were some differences generated by the use of the centrality measure, but there was no way of knowing which results were more valid.

In my data set, a calculation of correlation coefficients left no doubt that the incorporation of the additional concepts produced results successively more removed from the original

TABLE 3.1   Pearson Product-Moment Correlations Among Four
             Measures of Centrality

	Interlocks	Full Matrix	Strong Tie	Directional
Interlocks	—	.89	.71	.49
Full Matrix	.89	—	.84	.63
Strong Tie	.71	.84	—	.91
Directional	.49	.63	.91	—

frequency distributions. Table 3.1 presents a correlation matrix
of the relations among the various measures for 1904.

Interestingly, the correlation between number of interlocks
and full network centrality (.89) was almost identical to the .91
found by Mariolis. But, as we can see, the results diverge to the
point at which number of interlocks accounts for less than 25
percent of the variation in directional network centrality. Furthermore, similar results were found in all seven years. The
correlations between number of interlocks and directional centrality for the remaining six years were .53, .47, .46, .59, .64,
and .49.

Of course, knowing that a measure yields different results is
no assurance that those results are more meaningful. This is
particularly problematic with data from recent years, in which
there is a tremendous amount of controversy over the power of
various corporations, especially banks. However, nearly all
major observers, past and present, are in agreement about the
power of specific corporations around the turn of the century.
Hence, by examining what happens in the 1904 data when the
modifications are applied, we can gauge the validity of the
various measures of centrality.

There is a strong consensus that during this period the econ-
omy was dominated by a small group of powerful individuals.
Most notable among the leaders of this group were names such
as Morgan (J. P. Morgan & Co.), Rockefeller (Standard Oil),
Baker (First National Bank), Stillman (National City Bank),
Harriman (Union Pacific), and Schiff (Kuhn, Loeb & Co.).

TABLE 3.2   Twenty Most Interlocked Corporations, 1904

Rank	Name	Type	Number of Interlocks
1	National Bank of Commerce	Bank	153
2	Equitable Life Assurance	Insurance	107
3	U.S. Steel	Industrial	88
4	Mutual Life	Insurance	79
5	Baltimore & Ohio	Transport	76
6	Erie	Transport	76
7	New York Trust	Bank	75
8	Equitable Trust	Bank	74
9	Union Pacific	Transport	71
10	National City Bank	Bank	69
11	New York Central	Transport	68
12	New York Life	Insurance	62
13	Great Northern	Transport	58
14	U.S. Trust	Bank	58
15	Chicago & Alton	Transport	56
16	Chicago & Northwestern	Transport	53
16	Lehigh Valley	Transport	47
18	First National Bank (N.Y.)	Bank	45
19	Reading	Transport	45
20	International Harvester	Industrial	44

Railroads and industrial firms were both considered dependent on and subservient to financials during this period (see, for example, Noyes, 1909; Youngman, 1907; Moody, 1919; Corey, 1930; Josephson, 1934; Cochran and Miller, 1961; Carosso, 1970). Because of this, we should expect the most central firms of that period to be financials, and overall financial centrality to be higher than that of nonfinancials. I shall proceed in four steps, from the twenty most interlocked corporations to the twenty most central in the weighted strong tie (directional) network. Table 3.2 lists the twenty most interlocked firms.

TABLE 3.3   Twenty Most Central Corporations, 1904

Rank	Name	Type	Centrality Score
1	Erie	Transport	1.000
2	New York Central	Transport	.976
3	U.S. Steel	Industrial	.924
4	Baltimore & Ohio	Transport	.895
5	Great Northern	Transport	.871
6	National Bank of Commerce	Bank	.862
7	National City Bank	Bank	.832
8	First National Bank (N.Y.)	Bank	.801
9	New York Trust	Bank	.789
10	New York Life	Insurance	.788
11	International Harvester	Industrial	.783
12	Union Pacific	Transport	.782
13	Chicago & Alton	Transport	.774
14	Lehigh & Wilkes-Barre Coal	Industrial	.735
15	U.S. Trust	Bank	.708
16	Reading	Transport	.703
17	Chicago & Northwestern	Transport	.691
18	Mutual Life	Insurance	.687
19	Lehigh Valley	Transport	.687
20	Amalgamated Copper	Industrial	.667

Table 3.3 lists the twenty most central firms in the full network.

As we can see, the network is dominated by railroads and banks. The Erie Railroad, ranked sixth in number of interlocks (76), becomes the most central firm in the network on the basis of its interlocks with other highly interlocked firms. Meanwhile, the National Bank of Commerce, first in number of interlocks with 153, drops to sixth in centrality and Equitable Life, ranked second with 107 interlocks, drops out of the top 20 in centrality. The reason for this is that 18 of Equitable's interlocks are with its sister bank, Equitable Trust, and 14 are with the National Bank of Commerce. Hence, Equitable's impressive number of interlocks greatly overestimates its actual influence in the network. To return to Table 3.3, although the 20 corporations here include some of the most important firms of the period, the general character of the list bears little resemblance to what is known historically about the most important corporations at that time. Even the National Bank of Commerce was not a major independent power, but rather was dominated by J. P. Morgan and Thomas F. Ryan of Equitable (Sobel, 1965). Meanwhile, conspicuous by their absence are J. P. Morgan & Co., unquestionably the most powerful and influential firm of the period, and Kuhn, Loeb & Co., the second most powerful partnership in an era considered to be the heyday of investment banking.

The next step was to partition the matrix by eliminating the weak ties and recomputing the centrality scores. The list of the twenty most central firms in the strong tie network appears in Table 3.4. The changes are striking. J. P. Morgan & Co., ranked twenty-first in the full network, jumps to first in the strong tie, while Kuhn, Loeb, fiftieth in the full network, jumps to twentieth in the strong tie. At the same time, the descent of railroads and industrials is evident (both were considered subservient to banks at that time, as mentioned above). The Erie and the New York Central, first and second in the full matrix, drop to eighteenth and nineteenth, respectively, in the strong tie, reflecting the smaller amount of actual influence they held within the corporate world.

By accounting for the direction of interlocking we receive even more dramatic results. The 20 most central firms are listed in Table 3.5. Not only does Morgan maintain the top spot, but Kuhn, Loeb rises to twelfth, more accurately reflecting its influence in the economy. Two other important investment banks, Speyer & Co. and Winslow, Lanier & Co., also move into the top 20. The Erie and the New York Central are absent, as is U.S. Steel. The Erie had been in receivership a few years earlier before being bailed out by Morgan (Corey, 1930). The New

TABLE 3.4   Twenty Most Central Corporations, 1904 (Strong Tie Network)

Rank	Name	Type	Centrality Score
1	J. P. Morgan & Co.	Investment Bank	1.000
2	Great Northern	Transport	.906
3	New York Life	Insurance	.883
4	First National Bank (N.Y.)	Bank	.812
5	International Harvester	Industrial	.740
6	National City Bank	Bank	.701
7	U.S. Trust	Bank	.645
8	New York Trust	Bank	.610
9	Standard Oil	Industrial	.584
10	U.S. Steel	Industrial	.553
11	National Bank of Commerce	Bank	.530
12	Union Pacific	Transport	.515
13	Mutual Life	Insurance	.491
14	Title Guarantee and Trust	Bank	.488
15	Central Trust	Bank	.470
16	Chicago & Alton	Transport	.455
17	Amalgamated Copper	Industrial	.444
18	Erie	Transport	.404
19	New York Central	Transport	.403
20	Kuhn, Loeb & Co.	Investment Bank	.393

York Central was controlled by the Vanderbilts and was not itself a major independent power among corporations (Carosso, 1970). U.S. Steel, as is well known, was organized and remained under the strict control of J. P. Morgan for many years.

Overall, the strong tie and directional networks reflect the importance of financial institutions at the turn of the century. In the full network only seven of the twenty most central firms are financials, but in the directional network nine of the first twelve, and twelve of the first twenty, are financials. Further-

TABLE 3.5   Twenty Most Central Corporations, 1904 (Weighted Strong
              Tie [Directional] Network)

Rank	Name	Type	Centrality Score
1	J. P. Morgan & Co.	Investment Bank	1.000
2	New York Life	Insurance	.895
3	Great Northern	Transport	.783
4	International Harvester	Industrial	.685
5	U.S. Trust	Bank	.643
6	National City Bank	Bank	.610
7	First National Bank (N.Y.)	Bank	.601
8	Standard Oil	Industrial	.536
9	Central Trust	Bank	.528
10	Title Guarantee & Trust	Bank	.512
11	New York Trust	Bank	.504
12	Kuhn, Loeb & Co.	Investment Bank	.498
13	Chicago & Alton	Transport	.343
14	Union Pacific	Transport	.339
15	Mutual Life	Insurance	.329
16	Amalgamated Copper	Industrial	.318
17	Speyer & Co.	Investment Bank	.318
18	Winslow, Lanier & Co.	Investment Bank	.295
19	Rock Island	Transport	.272
20	Seaboard Air Line	Transport	.263

more, these highly central firms are considered the dominant
firms of the period. The National Bank of Commerce (ranked
twenty-third in the directional), one financial which declined
significantly in centrality, was not believed to have been an
independent financial force compared with James Stillman's
National City Bank (sixth), George F. Baker's First National
Bank (seventh), or John A. Stewart's U.S. Trust (fifth).

Table 3.6 shows the rank changes in the four ways of measuring centrality for selected corporations. The first four firms

TABLE 3.6   Rank on Four Centrality Measures

	Interlocks	Full	Strong Tie	Directional
J. P. Morgan & Co. (I)	38	21	1	1
Kuhn, Loeb & Co. (I)	80	50	20	12
Speyer & Co. (I)	88	67	39	17
Winslow, Lanier & Co. (I)	97	73	34	18
U.S. Steel (Z)	3	3	10	22
Baltimore & Ohio (T)	6	4	25	55
Erie (T)	7	1	18	47
Union Pacific (T)	8	12	12	14

NOTE: I = investment bank; Z = industrial; T = transport.

are the four most central investment banks, while the next five are the five most interlocked nonfinancial corporations. In all cases, the investment banks rise significantly as we incorporate the more sophisticated measures. Furthermore, the nonfinancial corporations, although highly central in the full network, decline sharply as the modifications are introduced. Also significant is the ascendence of Standard Oil, the Rockefeller creation. Standard leaps from thirty-fourth in the full matrix to ninth in the strong tie and eighth in the directional, more accurately reflecting its influence (and the Rockefellers' influence) in the economy.

In sum, the theoretically based modifications of the centrality measure produce results which lend powerful support to the validity of the measure. Corporations known to have been highly influential become more central as the more sophisticated measures are introduced. At the same time, heavily interlocked corporations which are known to have been controlled by and/or dependent on other corporations become successively less central. Because of its accurate reflection of relations in the corporate world in 1904, I shall refer primarily to the directional network in the comparative analysis of centrality.

Additional Comparative Techniques:
Connectivity

A major concern of this study is with the relative "tightness," or connectivity, of the networks for the various years. Network analysis has been accused, to some extent justifiably, of being static since it describes a set of relationships at one point in time. The historical approach used in this study is partly an attempt to rectify this problem.[4] Three types of connectivity will be considered here (for a discussion of these and other techniques, see Mitchell, 1969).

The first is the standard graph theory concept of density, based on the ratio of the number of connected lines in the graph to the number of all possible lines. This figure is essentially a measure of the frequency of social interaction among members of an interorganizational network. Following Durkheim (1933), we can postulate that the more intense the level of interaction, the higher the interdependence among the various units. Density can be expressed as $D_n = L_a/L_p$, where D_n = density of network N, L_a = actual number of connecting lines, L_p = possible number of connecting lines, and $L_p = n(n-1)/2$, where n = number of points.

This figure can be calculated for both the full and strong tie networks, with isolates (noninterlocked firms) either included or excluded. All possible variations will be calculated here.

The second measure of connectivity is the proportion of all board positions involving an interlock, or what I call the "interlocked position ratio" (IPR). This figure is a measure of the internal versus external orientation of corporate boards. The higher the IPR, the higher the proportion of board positions involving ties with other corporations. Of course, the IPR depends on the sizes of various boards. If certain corporations change the sizes of their boards so that different numbers of positions exist, this will affect the IPR without perhaps having any influence on intercorporate relationships. One way to deal with this is to simply count the numerator and ignore the denominator. This will be examined as well.

The third and final measure of connectivity is the number of points in the network that can be reached within a specified number of steps. Mitchell (1969) refers to this concept as "reachability," which I shall shorten to "reach."

This can be looked at in two ways, in terms of the "radius" and the "diameter." The radius is the percentage of firms that can be reached within a certain number of steps from the center, that being the most central corporation in the network. The diameter is the percentage of firms that can be reached within a certain number of steps from *any* corporation in the network. The more tightly connected the network, the greater the number of firms that can be reached in a small number of steps. Finally, as an additional criterion, the size and the number of components in the graph tell us something about the connectivity of the network.[5]

Interest Groups and Cliques

Among the issues most frequently studied in network analysis and its precursor, sociometry, is the existence of densely connected subgroups, or "cliques," within a larger population. In a 1939 study for the National Resources Committee (NRC), Paul M. Sweezy (1953) argued that the American economy was organized around a series of what he called "interest groups," or corporations under a common source of control. In the study of intercorporate relations, the concepts of cliques has been viewed as analogous to Sweezy's concept of interest group. Using interlocking directorates as a data source, studies by Dooley (1969), Levine (1972), Breiger et al. (1975), Bearden et al. (1975), Sonquist and Koenig (1976), and Allen (1978) have all assumed the clique-interest group similarity, although not always explicitly. But the relations between the two concepts have not been systematically explored. To complicate matters, each of the above studies employs a different technique of clique identification. At present, we not only lack a coherent concept of economic interest groups, but we also have complex and contradictory evidence of both their existence and their content.

In his original study, Sweezy (1953: 161) suggested that "companies ought to be grouped together if, in the absence of counterbalancing factors, they have a significant element of control in common."

Similarly, a later study coauthored by Sweezy defined interest groups as "a number of corporations under common control, the locus of power being normally an investment or commercial bank, or a great family fortune" (Baran and Sweezy, 1966: 17). This definition equates interest groups with financial or family control groups, that is, situations in which a particular financial institution or a wealthy family simultaneously controls several corporations. This would indicate that interest groups constitute hierarchical structures, dominated by a single corporation or family. In a financially based group, a bank controls several corporations simultaneously, attempting to maximize the profits of the group as a whole. J. P. Morgan, First National Bank, and Kuhn, Loeb & Co. were identified by Sweezy as leaders of financially based groups.

In family-based interest groups, a single corporation generally serves as the basis for the family empire. For example, a number of authors suggest that the foundation of the modern Rockefeller group is Chase Manhattan Bank, which is said to simultaneously control several other corporations (Elias, 1973; Knowles, 1973; Collier and Horowitz, 1976; Kotz, 1978; the Mellons and Du Ponts were identified by Sweezy as the other family-based groups). As in financially based groups, the subordinate corporations in the group are seen as tools for maximizing the profits of the group as a whole. Thus, from an interorganizational perspective, financial and family-based interest groups are similar in that both are hierarchical in character, and both tend to be dominated by a single firm.

But Sweezy (1953: 159) also identified groups which appeared to be based primarily on geographical similarity and community of interest. Indeed, he pointed out that the study sought to examine the extent to which corporations are linked through "community of interest groups, or more or less loose alliances." This definition suggests the possibility of relatively equalitarian groups not dominated by a single concern. However, among Sweezy's three geographically based groups, two (Cleveland and Boston) were in fact tied to specific concerns, Cleveland to the Mather family and Boston to the First National Bank (Boston)-Old Colony Trust. So seven of the eight groups originally defined by Sweezy were clearly hierarchical in character. Nevertheless, recent studies of interest groups based on interlocks have tended to apply techniques designed to generate nonhierarchical structures.

Using interlocking directorates for 250 large corporations from 1964, Dooley (1969) defined interest groups as densely connected sets of corporations. Groups were referred to as "tight-knit" if all firms had at least four interlocks with other firms in the group. "Loose-knit" groups were those in which firms interlocked two or three times with other group members. Using these criteria, Dooley found seven tight-knit and eight loose-knit groups, based primarily on geographical similarity.

Although this study represented a methodological advance, a number of problems remained. Not only were the original criteria for clique membership purely arbitrary, but Dooley (1969: 320) was forced to alter them for the New York based group: "So many corporations interlocked with the New York group that it was necessary to raise the cut-off point for membership in the group to six or more interlocks." Furthermore, Dooley's interpretation of his data suggests a lack of clarification surrounding the concept of interest groups. According to Dooley, only one group (the Mellons) was dominated by a family; the others "all [had] a local identity." Yet, later on, he points out that in most of the groups, "banks or life insurance companies form the central core of the group and have the greatest number of interlocks with other members of the group." Nevertheless, he fails to mention the possibility that the groups were financially based.

The next study to identify interest groups was conducted by Levine (1972). However, Levine's article was not an explicit attempt to detect interest groups, but was rather an illustration of a technique, multidimensional scaling, for the mapping of network structure. Employing a sample of 14 banks and 70 industrials from the Patman report (1968), Levine used a type of smallest space analysis known as nonmetric unfolding analysis. This involved setting up a matrix in which the distance between corporations was measured by the inverse of their number of directors in common. Thus, two firms with three shared directors were closer to one another than two firms with only one common director. These ties were mapped onto a two-dimensional "joint-space," which was raised to a third dimension in order to better approximate the relationships. This map was then modified by substituting spherical coordinates for rectangular ones. The result was a sphere-shaped map with several clusters centered around major banks. However, the results are unreliable because of the sample, which included only banks and industrials, from only three cities (New York, Chicago, and Pittsburgh). Furthermore, only the interlocks with banks were included in the input matrix. Interlocks between pairs of industrials were not included, strongly biasing the results toward high bank centrality.

Levine's data were reanalyzed by Breiger et al. (1975: 358-361), who employed the "CONCOR" blockmodeling algorithm to the 70 rows and 14 columns of the matrix. In this approach, a correlation matrix is constructed by correlating the columns of the original matrix. Then, in successive iterations, the columns of the matrix are correlated over and over, until the values converge toward 1 and −1. Those with high correlations with one another are grouped together. Because the matrix was not square, the rows (industrials) and the columns (banks) were clustered separately. In both cases, the corporations clustered along regional lines. The results were generally similar to Levine's, but were not completely comparable since the banks and industrials were clustered separately. As with Levine's article, the Breiger et al. piece was primarily methodological, and the authors did not attempt a substantive analysis of the data.

In a more theoretically oriented article, Sonquist and Koenig (1976) employed Alba's "n-clique" graph-theoretic approach (Alba, 1973) to detect interest groups. Using a set of 797 corporations from 1969 (Mariolis, 1975), the authors began by deleting all ties with fewer than 2 interlocks, producing a subset of 401 corporations. They then searched for groups in which each corporation was connected to all of the others. Groups with only 2 members were discarded, and any groups which differed from others by only a single firm were combined. Finally, groups were combined again if more than one-third of the members of a given smaller group were also members of a larger group. With these criteria, Sonquist and Koenig identified 32 cliques, ranging in size from 3 to 15 firms. As in the other studies, the cliques were based primarily on geographical similarity. "Almost all the cliques were composed solely or predominantly of firms headquartered in a single city or economic region" (Sonquist and Koenig, 1976: 72). The central roles within the groups appeared to be played by banks, but the authors' conclusions are ambiguous. They state that "in almost half of the cliques, a single bank played the financial role in the center" (p. 70), but it is not clear whether the bank was in a uniquely central position within the clique, or if it was merely the only bank in the clique.

Finally, the study by Allen (1978) made an explicit attempt to detect interest groups in the terms outlined by Sweezy. Using a sample of 250 corporations from 1935 and 1970, Allen employed direct factor analysis to identify interest groups. This involved squaring the original interlock matrix, and extracting the principal components from the squared matrix. Taking the 10 largest principal components from each of the 2 years, performing a varimax rotation, and including in the clique only those with loadings of .2 or higher, Allen found that the average size of the groups declined between the 2 periods, and that the proportion of interlocks with other group members relative to total interlocks also declined. Furthermore, Allen argued that the character of the groups had changed from those based primarily on family and financial ties to ones based primarily on geographical ties. This study was the first to distinguish explicitly the different types of groups, and is therefore the most theoretically relevant to the present study. Allen's analysis will form the starting point for the clique analysis in Chapter 6.

Discussion

The five studies discussed above all employ different methods of clique detection. Yet despite the different techniques, one common finding repeatedly appears: The principal characteristic of corporate cliques is their geographical character. Corporations within the same locale, with the possible exception of New York, tend to appear in the same groups. The fact that this result was produced consistently by the different studies suggests that it is a valid finding. Nevertheless, in this type of application, all five techniques are very similar in that they all share a particular conception of cliques and, hence, of interest groups.

The blockmodeling and factor analysis techniques (Breiger et al., Levine, Allen) all assume that cliques consist of elements that are "structurally equivalent" (or approximately so) with one another (MacRae, 1960; Lorrain and White, 1971). Two points are structurally equivalent if they have identical relations with all other points in the system. For example, if two companies both interlock with the same five other companies, they are considered structurally equivalent and are grouped together into the same clique.

But, interestingly, the graph-theoretic techniques (Dooley, Sonquist and Koenig) are based on the same principle. Corporations are grouped together if they have a certain number of ties *in common* with other points. The ideal-typical structure which is likely to emerge from this assumption is a clique in which every point is connected to every other point, as illustrated in Figure 3.1 for a hypothetical five-corporation clique. This configuration has one overriding characteristic: No one point is in a position to exercise either leadership or dominance over the others. The type of interest group most likely to approximate this structure would be a purely geographical group, in which corporations were linked together as coequals.

So, although the original concept of interest groups placed considerable emphasis on the particular domination of banks, the techniques discussed above are by their very nature unlikely to produce groups dominated by a single corporation. Even

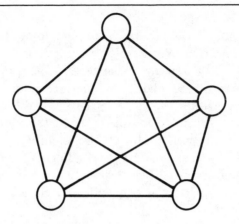

Figure 3.1 Hypothetical Nonhierarchical Clique

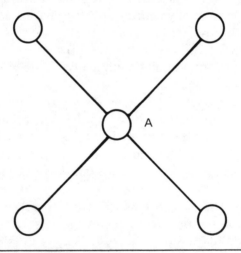

Figure 3.2 Hypothetical Hierarchical Clique

Levine's results, which appeared to signify bank dominance, were probably more a reflection of his data than of actual bank influence. If clearly bank-dominated groups actually existed, it is more likely that they would correspond to the classic wheel, or "X" form, as shown in Figure 3.2. In this structure, the central point (A) is in a strategically important position, since all communications between points must pass through A. As we have seen, a considerable amount of evidence exists to support the contention that this central point is in a unique position in terms of potential for leadership and influence. In sum, a technique capable of producing financial interest groups would have to consider ways of generating hierarchical structures similar to Figure 3.2.

Peak Analysis

One method designed to identify hierarchically based groups has been developed by Bearden et al. (1975) and Mariolis (1978). This approach, known as "peak analysis," is based on the Bonacich centrality measure. The first step in peak analysis involves determing the centrality of all corporations in the network. A peak is defined as a point which is more central than any point with which it directly interlocks. A point is a member of the clique defined by a particular peak if every more central point with which it interlocks is also a member of that clique. This can be expressed formally as

$$E_i \neq 0 \text{ iff } \forall_j, r_{ij} \neq 0 \rightarrow C_i > C_j \qquad [1]$$

$$j \in E_i \text{ iff } \forall_k, r_{jk} \neq 0 \text{ and } C_k > C_j \rightarrow K \in E_i \qquad [2]$$

where E_i = the clique associated with corporation i,

r_{ij} = measure of overlap (r_{ij} = 0 when no interlock occurs), and

C_i = centrality of corporation i.

The ideal-typical structure produced by this method is presented in Figure 3.3. A classic financially based interest group structure would be one in which several major banks were peaks, and corporations known to be under the banks' influence would be members of the respective cliques.

Notice also the existence of firms between two particular cliques. These "mixed members" are corporations tied to at

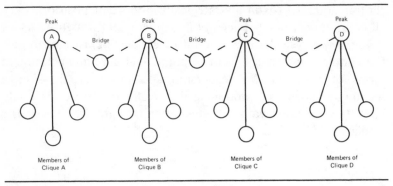

Figure 3.3 Ideal-Typical Peak Analysis Clique Structure

least two firms more central than they, both of which are in
different cliques. A "bridge," a type of mixed member, con-
nects two or more peaks. Peak analysis makes no assumptions
about the relations among non-peak members of a clique,
except that they be members of only that group. Structural
equivalence is not a basis for clique formation. Rather, being
under the purview of a specific peak is the sole criterion.

ADVANTAGES AND LIMITATIONS OF PEAK ANALYSIS

Peak analysis appears to have several advantages over the
other approaches for the identification of corporate interest
groups. First, rather than incorporating the structural equivalence assumption, which, as we have seen, may be inappropriate
here, peak analysis is more likely to produce a group structure
commensurate with financially based interest groups. Second,
peak analysis provides the possibility for any number of cliques,
of any size. The method is entirely objective, involving no
judgment decisions by the researcher. It is therefore "refut-
able," that is, unlike the other approaches, it is possible that
separate cliques will not be identified. Blockmodel analysis
allows for the possibility of hypothesis testing, but even here a
decision must be made concerning the minimum level of density
necessary to constitute a "oneblock" (see Arabie and Boorman,
1977). Third, unlike factor analysis, although similar to the

graph-theoretic and blockmodel approaches, peak analysis provides a concept of mixed membership, when corporations are close to two or more groups but are not clearly members of any one. Thus, it provides a view of the entire network, rather than of only the cliques. Fourth, peak analysis is based on the theoretically sophisticated concept of centrality.

Ironically, the very strengths of peak analysis are the sources of some of its weaknesses. Because of its stringent criteria for clique membership, the method may be overly restrictive. Studies of interlocks have produced a finding that Fennema and Schijf (1979: 319) refer to as "strikingly monotonous": one large, completely connected graph. This increases the likelihood that in a peak analysis only one huge clique will be identified. And, indeed, this is what has been found in studies by Bearden et al. (1975) and Mariolis (1978), as well as in the present study. This finding may in itself be important, especially since the Bearden et al. study found meaningful groupings when taking the strength and direction of ties into account. But an additional problem remains, namely, the extreme sensitivity of the measure to even minute fluctuations in the centrality scores. As I pointed out above, the scores are themselves only estimates, subject to varying amounts of measurement error. And yet the smallest alteration in one score can have a major effect on the structure of the cliques. For example, imagine that firm A, with a score of .335, is a member of clique B, based on its interlock with firm C (centrality of .336). If A interlocks with 25 less-central firms, all of which are tied only to each other or to A, then all 25 firms would be members of clique B. But what if A's score was .3361 instead of .335, entirely plausible given the normal range of error? In that case, the 25 firms would all be members of a *separate* clique defined by A, and C would become a mixed member between cliques A and B. Such minor differences in centrality scores appear too trivial to have such major consequences attached to them. Thus, peak analysis, while containing advantages over the other approaches on substantive grounds, may have disadvantages on technical grounds.

The best way to resolve this issue is to directly compare the results produced by the different approaches. In Chapter 6, a comparison between the results produced by Allen's (1978) factor analysis and the peak analysis from the present study will be discussed.

Summary

The preceding discussion has outlined the various techniques to be used in analyzing the data. It was argued that the centrality measure based on strong tie interlocks weighted for directionality provides the most accurate indicator of network influence. Measures of connectivity for the comparative analysis of networks over time were discussed. Finally, I discussed the concept of interest groups, and their translation into cliques in network analysis. This was followed by a discussion of the relative merits of the various approaches to clique identification.

The following chapter will describe the focus of the data analysis, including various hypotheses, discussions of what we can expect to find given the managerialist thesis, and the meanings associated with those findings.

NOTES

1. Parts of the following discussion are adapted from Mizruchi and Bunting (1981).

2. Early in the century, a number of individuals were officers of two or more firms simultaneously. Whenever this occurred, all ties involving the officership were coded as strong ties. Thus, the crucial determinant of the strength of a tie in this study is whether the interlock involves an officer.

3. The reader will notice that this modification produces an asymmetric matrix with different eigenvectors depending on whether the column or row correlations are treated. In this case, the largest eigenvector based on summing the correlation coefficients in the columns of the matrix (in which $W_s = .9$) is employed as the vector of centrality scores. The largest eigenvector based on the coefficients in the rows could also be used, but this would necessarily involve different theoretical assumptions since the weights would be reversed (W_s would equal .1). It should also be noted that the definition used here differs slightly from that used by both Bearden et al. and Mintz. The denominator used in their models was $\sqrt{d_j}$, on the grounds that

the sender's influence at the receiving firm was based only on the percentage of directors at the receiver which represented the former. However, in order to be consistent with our previous definition of r_{ij} we must account not only for the proportion of directors at the receiving firm, but also for the receiving firm's ability to send, which is based on the size of *its* board. In any case, a run of 1904 data using both measures yielded only minor and insignificant differences.

4. The only existing historical analysis of density was done by Stanworth and Giddens (1975) on British data, although comparative analyses over very recent years have also been conducted (see Fennema and Schijf, 1979, for references).

5. A "component" is a set of completely connected points in which any point A can be reached from any point B in X number of steps, where X is a finite number greater than 0.

CHAPTER 4

TESTING THE MANAGERIALIST THESIS

Early studies of corporate interlocks, including those by the congressional committees and by Warner and Unwalla (1967), Dooley (1969), Levine (1972), and Bearden et al. (1975), were almost purely descriptive in that they were concerned with delineating the characteristics associated with interlocks, rather than testing hypotheses about corporate behavior. More recently, studies by Mariolis (1975), Sonquist and Koenig (1976), and Mintz (1978) have attempted to relate interlocks more specifically to questions of corporate control. But even these studies are not in fact testing "theories," but rather are examining the accuracy of various descriptions of society. Underlying these studies is the assumption that they will provide an empirical basis upon which various theories can be developed (see Levine, 1977).

The most sophisticated theoretical approach to the study of interlocking directorates is that of the resource dependence school discussed above. Researchers within this framework have developed a number of hypotheses on the relation between interlocks and various characteristics of corporations. However, as we have seen, the evidence in support of this position is only moderately significant.

The present study is to a great extent descriptive. I am particularly concerned with understanding the shape and content of intercorporate relations in the early 1900s, what changes have occurred, and how the present structure resembles the earlier one. Nevertheless, as we have seen, the managerialist thesis is based on several assumptions about the changing nature of intercorporate relations in the twentieth-century United States. Thus, although much of the data analysis presented in this study will be of a descriptive nature, a considerable portion will be devoted to an examination of several hypotheses as well. This chapter maps out the specific areas of inquiry, and discusses the hypotheses to be examined.

Areas of Focus

In the most general terms, this study focuses on changes in the structure of intercorporate relations in the American economy from 1904 to 1974. The hypotheses examined will be based on what I will call "pure managerialism," the position discussed in Chapter 1. Cases in which other managerialist interpretations (such as the cooptation model) are possible will be identified and the alternative formulations discussed. The specific focus of the study will be on three major areas:

(1) connectivity of the network
(2) centrality of various sectors
(3) changing clique formations

CONNECTIVITY

Interlocks. The degree to which a corporation is interlocked can be viewed as a measure of its interdependence with other corporations. We would expect the less interlocked firm to be more competitive and have fewer common interests with other corporations than the heavily interlocked firm. On a system level, we would expect a heavily interlocked system to have more overall cohesion and interdependence than a lightly interlocked one. This point was suggested by Arnold Rose (1967: 123) when he stated that "interlocking directorates, where they occur in the larger corporations, give them a high degree of cohesiveness." Rose (1967: 92), in fact, believed that interlocks were uncommon, "the exception rather than the rule." While it is not possible to determine exactly how many interlocks would constitute the rule and how few would indicate an exception, we can compare the frequency of interlocking at various points in time. Studies by Dooley (1969) and Allen (1974) found roughly equal numbers of interlocks between 1935 and 1965 and 1970, respectively. Bunting and Barbour (1971) found that interlocking between 1896 and 1964 had declined considerably, which would appear to support the managerialist thesis.

Similarly, if corporations are increasingly controlled by insiders, we should expect to see fewer and fewer outsiders on their boards (Dooley, 1969). If external control of corporations is a declining phenomenon, we should observe fewer instances of corporations linked together by external ties of either ownership or board control. Thus, the first hypothesis of this study is that:

(1) The number of interlocks in the system has declined over time.

A finding of no decline or an increase in interlocking could also be consistent with the cooptation model. According to this model, intercorporate alliances are created to serve a specific organizational imperative. If corporations have become more successful in dealing with their environments, this might be reflected in a high level of cooptation, and hence an increase in interlocking. But the cooptation model is an attempt to explain the behavior of particular organizations, not that of inter-organizational systems. There is nothing in this model to suggest that interlocking among large corporations has either increased or decreased over time. Thus, any result on Hypothesis 1 could be interpreted in a way consistent with the cooptation model. To the extent that no decline in interlocking is consistent with the cooptation model, the model represents a departure from traditional managerialism. An increase in interlocking is indicative of increased interdependence within the system, regardless of the motives leading to the establishment of the interlocks.

Density. Since the network density is to a large extent based on the amount of interlocking, we might expect changes in density to parallel those of interlocking. However, there is an important distinction between the two based on the distribu-

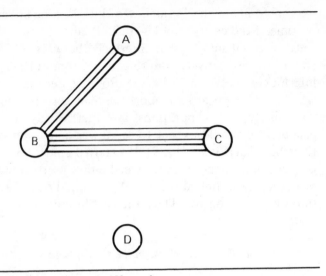

Figure 4.1 Sparse, Heavily Interlocked Network
NOTE: In all figures, each line represents a separate interlock.

tion of interlocking in the system. It is possible for a system to have more interlocks than another and yet be less dense. To take an extreme example, consider a system with four points, A, B, C, and D. Suppose A and B share three directors and B and C share five directors (as in Figure 4.1). Despite the eight interlocks in the system, the density is only .33, since only two of the six possible connections actually occur. Now consider the same system at a different point in time. Suppose A has one interlock apiece with B and D, B one with C, and C one with D (as in Figure 4.2). This system now has only four interlocks, but a density of .66. Despite only half as many interlocks, it is actually twice as dense.

Thus, although the measure of density does not account for the strength of the connections between any two points, it gives a more accurate indicator of overall network connectivity than does the number of interlocks. Density is often employed as a measure of group cohesiveness in sociometric analysis. If corporations are highly interdependent, then network density should be relatively high. Since the managerialist argument

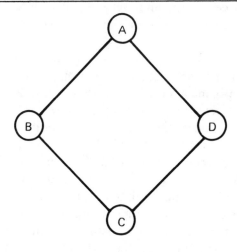

Figure 4.2 Dense, Lightly Interlocked Network

suggests that corporations are becoming more and more
independent, the predicted changes in density should be similar
to those of interlocking. By using both measures, we will be
better able to analyze the specific content of the changes.
Furthermore, the two other variants of density discussed in
Chapter 3, the interlocked position ratio and the reach, would
be expected to behave in a similar fashion. Thus, three more
hypotheses can be derived:

(2) *The density of the network has declined over time.*
(3) *The proportion of board positions involving an interlock has
declined over time.*
(4) *The number of corporations that can be reached within a small
number of steps has declined over time.*

As an additional note, Hypothesis 3 corresponds to another
aspect of the managerialist perspective: the growing importance
and power of those with technical expertise (Galbraith, 1967;
Bell, 1973). The more significance attached to those with
specialized knowledge, the more likely that a board will be
composed of insiders. The IPR is an indirect indicator of this,
since we can assume that the more specific one's knowledge, the

less likely one is to interlock, especially considering that multiple directorships within the same industry are in most cases illegal.

Centrality of various sectors. As mentioned in Chapter 1, a particularly important element of the managerialist view is the idea that nonfinancial corporations have become better able to finance investment with internally generated funds, thus freeing them from dependence on financial corporations. If this actually is the case, then we should observe several changes in the pattern of interlocking between financials and nonfinancials.

But before continuing, the term *financial* must be discussed. As Mariolis (1975) has pointed out, there has been much confusion associated with this term. Financial corporations include commercial banks, investment banks, and insurance companies. Financial control theorists have posited situations of both bank control and bank and insurance company control, and have often been contradictory on the subject. To alleviate potential confusion, financial corporations will be treated both separately and as a group. This is important because the roles of various sectors of the financial community have changed during the course of the twentieth century. If the managerialist position is correct, we should expect to observe several trends. The hypotheses are as follows:

> *(5) The number of interlocks between financials and nonfinancials has declined over time (Allen, 1974: 402-403).*
> *(6) The centrality of financials has declined over time.*
> *(7) The number of financials among the most central corporations has declined over time.*

Furthermore, if financials have become progressively less powerful and nonfinancials progressively more powerful, then we should expect to observe changes in the direction of financial interlocking. As financials become less dominant, they are less likely to have as high a percentage of sending interlocks.

> *(8) The ratio of sending to total interlocks for financials has declined over time.*[1]

(9) Financial centrality in the directional network has declined relative to financial centrality in the full and strong tie networks.

Finally, although this discussion has focused mainly on financial corporations, it can be viewed within the larger structure of the modified resource dependence model presented above. That is, corporations whose resources are particularly significant and highly demanded at a given point in time should become highly central in the corporate network. If the need for financial capital has declined, then financial centrality should have declined. This proposition is extremely difficult to test since it may lead to circular reasoning, that is, which corporations are highly central? The ones which control the most important resources. How do we know which firms control the most important resources? By their centrality. Until we have a means of measuring the specific demand for a variety of resources in the economy at a given time, we cannot test this hypothesis. Burt (1979; Burt et al., 1980) has begun such a measurement by attempting to derive the importance of specific resources to members of various sectors in the economy. His results appear to support this view. In this study I will attempt to evaluate the proposition by analyzing the fluctuations in centrality among various sectors, and of various industries within the industrial and transportation sectors.

At the same time, a related hypothesis about the role of financials can be evaluated. In the finance capital perspective, one of the sources of the power of financials is their ability to shift capital in and out of various sectors. Both its flexibility and the fact that capital is a universal resource presumably give financials a disproportionate share of power. If, as the managerialists argue, external sources of capital are no longer as highly demanded by nonfinancials, and if major nonfinancial corporations have attained a certain degree of permanence and stability, then we should expect the relative stability of financials to have declined. That is, we should expect less persistence of a particular set of financials among the most central corporations as the century progresses.

(10) The relative stability of the most central financials versus the most central nonfinancials has declined over time.[2]

As mentioned above, the decline and ascendence of other sectors will be related to historical developments in order to provide suggestive evidence with which to assess the resource dependence view.

Changes in clique formation. In his analysis of 1935 data, Sweezy argued that the economy was organized in a series of interest groups, of which he identified eight. Although it was not made explicit, the implication was that this situation had existed at least since the beginning of the twentieth century. However, most of the literature about the period around 1900 suggests either that there were two major groups, Morgan and Rockefeller (see Youngman, 1907), or that there were in fact no distinct groups (Moody, 1919). Since no actual clique analysis has been done on data prior to 1935, this study will provide the first systematic analysis of cliques in this earlier period.

The empirical literature on changing clique formations is scarce. Perlo (1957) used a variety of sources to compare cliques in the mid 1950s with those designated by Sweezy for 1935. He found a high level of stability, arguing that six of Sweezy's eight groups remained in 1955, while two groups identified by Sweezy had been replaced by two others. Dooley (1969) identified interest groups from 1964 interlock data (see Chapter 3) and also argued that the groups remained very similar in content. However, only the study by Allen (1978) has directly compared cliques across time by analyzing two sets of data with identical techniques.

Using factor analysis (see Chapter 3), Allen compared the ten most cohesive interlock groups from 1935 and 1970. He found several changes. First, the average size of the cliques declined from 10.0 members in 1935 to 6.6 in 1970. Second, the cliques were generally less cohesive in 1970, corporations maintaining a smaller percentage of their interlocks within their cliques (33.7 percent in 1970 compared with 41.8 percent in 1935). Third, there was a decline in the number of groups based on financial ties (from 4 to 2) and a corresponding increase in the number based primarily on geographical ties. In 1970, a significantly smaller percentage of corporations could be placed in cliques (25.7 percent compared with 33.3 percent in 1935), and an even smaller percentage of all interlocks occurred within cliques (16.8 percent compared with 39.7 percent in 1935). Since the total number of interlocks is about the same in both periods, Allen (1978: 611) concludes that the "corporate elite structure" has become "more diffuse and less concentrated." Thus, the system is seen as concentrated if several large, cohesive cliques exist. As the cliques become smaller and less cohesive, the system becomes more diffuse.

The problem here is the failure to distinguish between concentration at the local level and concentration at the national level. It is entirely possible that the disintegration of cliques might lead to an increase in concentration of power at the level of the system as a whole. Centralization in several local areas suggests a decentralization at the national level. A blurring of distinctions among local centers of power may indicate a growing centralization of power at the national level.

The question is how to measure this centralization. One way, in fact employed by Allen in an earlier article (Allen, 1974), is to chart the distribution of interlocking in the system. In doing this, Allen found that the distribution became more equal between 1935 and 1970. However, this gives us only part of the picture. Let us compare two figures. Figure 4.3 is a five-corporation network in which all five firms have two interlocks. This system is highly decentralized, since no one corporation is in a position to dominate the others. But compare this with the situation in Figure 4.4. Here we again have a case in which all five corporations have two interlocks apiece. However, the situation is far different. In this case, firm A sends representatives to firms B and C, which in turn send representatives to D and E, while D and E share a neutral interlock. This situation leads one to expect that firm A would exert a disproportionate share of influence. The measure of centrality using the direc-

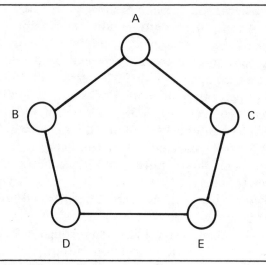

Figure 4.3 Decentralized Network

tional criteria would account for the uniqueness of this situation, while counting only the number of interlocks would treat
this case as identical with Figure 4.3. Thus, examining the
distribution of centrality scores over time might help alleviate
the defects of focusing only on the number of ties.

We are now in a position to list three hypotheses about
changing clique formations derived from the above discussion:

(11) Cliques have disintegrated over time.

This hypothesis is based on changes in the number of cliques,
the number of clique members, and their relative cohesiveness
(density and centrifugality), all of which would decline, according to the managerialist thesis. Given the discussion above, the
disintegration of cliques per se is not sufficient to demonstrate a
decline of centralized power. For the managerialist argument to
be supported, it is necessary for the level of concentration
within the system as a whole to have declined. Thus:

*(12) The distribution of interlocking has become more equal over
time.*

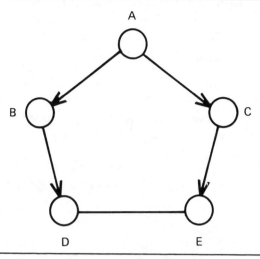

Figure 4.4 Centralized Network

(13) The distribution of centrality has become more equal over time.

The distribution will be analyzed in terms of both interlocking and centrality for two reasons: (1) in order to directly examine Allen's hypothesis; and (2) to compare the results of the centrality analysis with those of the interlock analysis.

Even with these two hypotheses, it should be pointed out that the dispersal of particular interest groups might be accompanied by a reintegration of corporations on a larger level. In this case, the dispersal of specific groups would be the precursor to the increased unity of the system as a whole. While a lower level of centralization is consistent with the managerialist thesis, the existence of group overlap on a systemwide level would suggest a general community of interest within the corporate world.

The fourth hypothesis regarding cliques is based on their character as either financial or geographical interest groups. The managerialist position is that, to the extent that interest groups continue to exist, they are less likely to be dominated by either families or financial corporations, and are more likely to be

groups of coequals based on geographical proximity, with no
one firm dominating the others. Thus, the internal hierarchy of
the cliques would be expected to decline. Based on this argument, the final hypotheses are as follows:

(14) *Cliques have become based less on financial ties than on
geographical ties.*
(15) *The prevalence of financial corporations as peaks has declined
over time.*

The hypotheses will be analyzed in terms of peak analysis and
then compared with the results of Allen's factor analysis.

INDEPENDENT CRITERIA

A major problem with studies of interlocking directorates has
been the absence of systematic, reliable independent evidence
with which to compare interlocks. As a result, much of the
external data available are applied post hoc and hence cannot be
employed in hypothesis testing. The present study confronts
similar problems, in particular because of its historical nature. It
is virtually impossible to develop testable hypotheses on testimony before congressional committees, or on stock or loan data
that are available only in fragments. Nevertheless, enough of
this evidence is available so that illustrations which enrich the
quantitative findings can be brought to bear. Since this information, particularly that on corporate control, is sometimes of
questionable reliability, I have sought a plurality of sources at
all possible points. We are fortunate in one thing: While in
recent years there is more systematic evidence available, particularly with stock ownership data, the earlier years contain more
explicit, detailed, and consistent qualitative data. I have included this independent evidence wherever possible.

The following chapter will provide a general description of
the corporate world during the early twentieth century, examining Hypotheses 1-10, developed in this chapter. At the same
time, an attempt will be made to account specifically for the
factors that led to the observed changes. Then Chapter 6 will

analyze the changes in clique formation, including a comparison of the two methods discussed in Chapter 3.

NOTES

1. In the cooptation model, a decrease in the ratio of financial sending to receiving interlocks would suggest an increasing ability of financials to coopt elements of their external environments. This would suggest an increase in financial influence, a finding contrary to the managerialist thesis.

2. One reader has remarked that "it does not necessarily follow that managerialism would expect intercorporate connections to be constantly shifting. If intercorporate relations stem from corporate needs, [they] would shift only insofar as needs are changing. There are many needs that are sustained. In fact, most of the 'needs' that the cooptation perspective posits are fairly constant" (William G. Roy, personal communication). But what if one resource is more critical than others? If one sector or industry possesses a set of resources which consistently stands out as crucial to corporate survival, then the system will assume a hierarchical character, dominated by those who control this critical resource. If investment capital is a consistently important resource over time, then banks will assume a disproportionately influential position within the system. This view is directly contrary to the managerialist thesis.

CHAPTER 5

THE CORPORATE NETWORK

*Interlocking Directorates
and the Rise of Big Business*

The first major development of interlocking directorates in the United States occurred between 1870 and 1900. In a study of interlocks among the 55 largest railroads, banks, and insurance companies, Bunting (1979) found that from 1871 to 1902 interlocks among these companies increased nearly fivefold (from 116 to 545). The largest increase, from 204 to 545, took place between 1891 and 1902. This occurred despite the fact that the sectoral concentration ratios did *not* increase during this period. Bunting concludes from this that the fear of large corporations in the United States around the turn of the century stemmed not from their increasing monopolization, but rather from the apparent concentration of control. During the 1871-1902 period, the number of different individuals directing these 55 corporations declined from 847 to 759, while the number of actual board positions increased from 941 to 1028.

This 30-year period corresponded with a period of rapid industrialization and expansion of the American economy. It was during this era that many of the leading capitalists (known as the "Robber Barons") acquired their great wealth. These people included Jay Gould, Jay Cooke, Cornelius Vanderbilt, and later Edward H. Harriman in railroads and John D. Rockefeller in petroleum. By the 1890s, John Pierpont Morgan was putting together the financial system that, by virtually all accounts, would rule the economy at least through World War I.

By 1900, the United States had entered the "era of finance capital" (Cochran and Miller, 1961), in which railroads and industrials became increasingly dependent on financials, particularly investment banks, for the capital necessary for continued expansion. One reason for the power of financials was the bankruptcy suffered by many railroads in the depression of 1893, which placed the railroads at the mercy of the banks. The leader of railroad reorganization was J. P. Morgan, who was guided by three principles:

> First, to guarantee solvency for the future, fixed charges must be reduced to a figure that could be met under all conditions, with the payment of dividends on common stock relatively of minor importance. Second, a general "community of interest" must be established among major companies so that costly competition would be replaced by cooperation. Third, the House of Morgan must dominate the boards of directors of the reorganized companies. In the creation of the Southern Railway System, in the reorganization of the Erie, Baltimore & Ohio, Reading, and almost any other railroad in which Morgan was interested, the *last two* of these principles were religiously observed [Cochran and Miller, 1961: 196-197; emphasis in original].

Two points are of note here. First, Morgan was less concerned with dividends paid on common stock than with getting the company on a strong footing. Thus, he did not control a corporation merely to extract dividends on large blocks of stock. Second, placing representatives on the boards of various companies was the mechanism by which Morgan exercised control. This is clearly illustrated by the boards of two Morgan creations, U.S. Steel and International Harvester. Not only did Morgan place three representatives on the boards of both companies (including two of the three members of the Harvester finance committee), but the Pujo Committee hearings revealed that every member of the original U.S. Steel board was first approved by Morgan (Corey, 1930: 275).

In the early part of this century, interlocking directorates were widely viewed as mechanisms of corporate control in this manner. So dangerous were they considered that the Clayton Act of 1914 specifically outlawed interlocks between competing companies within particular industries.

THE NETWORK IN 1904

In Chapter 3, it was demonstrated that as we moved from measures of the absolute number of interlocks to those of the weighted strong tie network, the data came more and more to resemble most historical accounts of corporate power in the early twentieth century. The most central corporations were in most cases those which were considered most important during that time, including J. P. Morgan & Co., the First National Bank, Standard Oil, National City Bank, and Kuhn, Loeb & Co.

But the entire system was heavily interlocked. In 1904, there was a total of 1531 separate interlocks among the 166 corporations, an average of 18.4 per firm. There were 16 corporations with more than 50 interlocks apiece, and 37 had more than 30 interlocks. Only 12 firms had no interlocks. The remaining 154 formed one continuous graph. Starting at the center of the graph, 28.8 percent of the firms could be reached within one step, 83.0 percent within two, and 98.0 percent within three steps. The most heavily interlocked sectors were railroads and banks, with averages of 37.4 and 37.2 interlocks per firm, respectively. Industrials (10.4) and investment banks (6.3) were the least interlocked. However, in the centrality analysis, the railroads declined in importance while the banks and investment banks increased. Kuhn, Loeb & Co., with only 10 interlocks, is the twelfth most central corporation in the directional analysis, while the Baltimore & Ohio, with 76 interlocks, is the fifty-fifth most central.

Overall, the picture of the network in 1904 corresponds with the view of the corporate world described by historians and social scientists. The network is tightly connected and is dominated by corporations associated with the interests of the major capitalists of the period, in particular Morgan (J. P. Morgan & Co.), Baker (First National Bank), Rockefeller (Standard Oil), Stillman (National City Bank), and Schiff (Kuhn, Loeb & Co.;

Corey, 1930; Allen, 1935; Moody, 1919; Youngman, 1907; Redlich, 1951; Josephson, 1934; Carosso, 1970).

Direct lines of control were in evidence as well. U.S. Steel and International Harvester, two companies formed and controlled by Morgan, received three and two directors from Morgan, respectively. Morgan partners George W. Perkins and Charles Steele, as well as Morgan himself, sat on the board of U.S. Steel. Perkins and Steele also sat on the board of International Harvester, and Perkins and Morgan ally H. P. Davison were among Harvester's three voting trustees. Morgan partners also sat on the boards of nine major railroads, only one of which (Baltimore & Ohio) was not considered under Morgan control at the time. Similar patterns could be found among Rockefeller-dominated Amalgamated Copper, which received two directors from Standard Oil, and the Chicago and Alton, part of a struggle for control between Harriman (five directors from Harriman's Union Pacific) and the Moores (four directors from the Moores' Rock Island).

Another important characteristic of the period was the presence of a few powerful individuals, whose interests transcended those of the corporations with which they were affiliated. There were 24 individuals with 6 or more directorships within the 166-firm sample. Many of these people were either defined as "independent capitalists," not principally affiliated with any one organization, or were officers of more than one firm simultaneously, a phenomenon virtually nonexistent in more recent years. Among these 24 individuals, only 11 could be clearly identified with a particular corporation within the sample. These included J. P. Morgan (8 directorships), J. H. Hyde, Vice President of Equitable Life Assurance (10), and James Stillman, President of National City Bank (13). There were 6 people who held officerships in two or three firms in the sample, including George F. Baker, President of First National Bank (and an officer of the Great Northern Railroad and Mutual Life Insurance), H. H. Rogers (Standard Oil, Amalgamated Copper, and Mutual), and George W. Perkins (J. P. Morgan & Co., New York Life Insurance, and International Harvester). Thus, the prev-

TABLE 5.1   Mean Number of Interlocks

Sector	1904	1912	1919	1935	1964	1969	1974
Industrials	10.4	10.9	8.7	6.4	7.8	8.9	8.3
Transports	37.4	33.6	20.8	11.8	8.4	6.9	4.8
Insurances	27.5	14.4	14.6	13.2	15.9	14.4	12.0
Investment Banks	6.3	7.6	5.7	2.2	2.9	2.5	0.8
Banks	37.2	43.2	21.4	15.8	17.0	19.4	16.7
Total	18.4	18.1	12.1	8.5	9.1	9.7	8.5

alent view of the period as one in which corporations were dominated by a few individuals is reflected in the interlock analysis.

I shall now turn to the hypotheses discussed in Chapter 4 to chart the extent to which this situation has changed. In this chapter I will concentrate on two areas: (1) connectivity of the network; and (2) the relative centrality of various sectors, especially financials.

Connectivity

Table 5.1 presents the mean number of interlocks for each of the seven years, broken down by sector. The number of interlocks in the system was highest in 1904, remained high in 1912, and then underwent a significant decline between 1912 and 1935. Between 1935 and the 1964-1974 period, interlocking increased slightly. The first hypothesis discussed in Chapter 4 relates to the decline in the prevalence of interlocking consistent with the managerialist position of growing corporate independence. To examine this hypothesis, I performed a one-tailed t-test between given pairs of years, treating time as the independent variable and number of interlocks as the dependent variable. According to Hypothesis 1, interlocking should decline over time.[1] This hypothesis was examined for the six intervals between the years for which data are available. The results of the t-test are presented in Table 5.2.

These findings support the managerialist hypothesis between 1912 and 1919 and from 1919 to 1935. During those two periods, there was a statistically significant decline in the mean number of interlocks. However, after 1935 there was no significant change. In fact, there were increases from 1935 to 1969, although in 1974 interlocking again drops back to the 1935 level. Thus, the managerialist position is given partial support by the data.[2]

There is some question whether the sharp decline in interlocking between 1912 and 1919 was actually a result of legislation rather than an actual tendency toward growing corporate independence. As noted above, the Clayton Act of 1914 outlawed interlocks between competing firms. As Bunting (1977) has shown, the number of interlocks between competitors that were broken between 1912 and 1919 accounts for a considerable portion of the decline in total interlocking (see Chapter 7). However, there are at least three reasons why the decline between 1912 and 1919 should be viewed as supporting managerialism.

First, the amount of interlocking in the system continued its sharp decline between 1919 and 1935, suggesting that processes other than the Clayton Act were at work. Second, the Clayton Act can itself be viewed as part of the historical process leading to managerial control. There are two parts to the managerialist thesis, the descriptive (or factual) element and the causal ele-

TABLE 5.2   Changes in Interlocking

Year Interval	t-value	d.f.	p
1904-1912	0.13	331	.894
1912-1919	3.20	332	.001*
1919-1935	3.28	332	.0005*
1935-1964	−0.71	332	.240
1964-1969	−0.67	332	.252
1969-1974	1.48	332	.070

* Significant at .01 level; negative t-values indicate an increase in interlocking.

ment. The descriptive element involves the extent to which managerialism provides an accurate account of the changes in corporate control during the twentieth century; in other words, whether what managerialists say happened has actually happened. The causal element involves the sources of these developments; in other words, the reasons why the managerial revolution took place. While the causal element is obviously important, it is secondary to and contingent on the factual basis of the managerialist thesis. My major concern here is whether the managerial revolution in fact occurred. Only after this question is answered can one look for its causes. Thus, if the legislation prohibiting interlocking between competitors contributed to the growth of management control, then the law must be viewed as part of the historical process of managerialism, not as external to it. Finally, there was an equally important factor in the decline of interlocking between 1912 and 1919: the decline of multiple-interlocked individuals. The consequences of this decline were not necessarily those suggested by managerialists, as I point out in Chapter 7. But the sources of this trend had little to do with the Clayton Act.

Sectoral changes. Although this issue is considered in greater detail below, it is interesting to note the changes within the sectors. Between 1904 and 1974, the relative positions of industrials and transports reversed themselves. While industrial interlocking declined only slightly, and actually increased after 1935, transport interlocking declined consistently and sharply during the period. None of the declines in industrial interlocking are statistically significant. Transport interlocking, on the other hand, sustained significant decreases between 1912 and 1919, 1919 and 1935, and 1935 and 1964. While banks remained the most interlocked sector from 1912 on, bank interlocking declined significantly between 1912 and 1919. Trends in transport and bank interlocking tend to mirror those of interlocking as a whole from 1912 to 1935. However, after 1935, transport interlocking continued to decline while bank interlocking stabilized and then increased slightly. Insurance company interlocking dropped considerably between 1904 and

1912 (although the decline is not statistically significant), probably as a result of the Armstrong Investigation of 1905 into
illegal practices and the subsequent legislation requiring insurance companies to dispose of bank and trust company stocks
(Keller, 1963). However, after 1912 insurance company interlocking remained basically stable. Finally, investment banks,
although never as involved in interlocking as the other sectors,
still showed a decline from 1912 on, although only between
1919 and 1935 was the decline statistically significant. By
1974, investment banks had virtually no involvement in
interlocking.

NETWORK DENSITY

In Chapter 3 I outlined three different measures of network
density: the traditional graph theory definition, the interlocked
position ratio (IPR), and the "reach," or radius of the graph.
Hypotheses 2 through 4 are based on an implicit managerialist
position that these three indicators of connectivity would decline through time. Unfortunately, the nature of these data is
such that these hypotheses are not amenable to statistical testing. Therefore, I shall report the results and assess the extent to
which they appear significant. Table 5.3 provides a picture of
the ratio of connected lines to all possible connections, based
on both the full and strong tie networks, and for both the entire
graph and only the connected points.
    The network density follows very closely the pattern of
interlocking, although the decline between 1912 and 1935 is
not as sharp. The main exception is between 1904 and 1912,
when the number of interlocks declined while the full network
density increased. This was the result of a considerable decline
in the number of interlocks per tie, from 1.56 to 1.44. In later
years, this ratio continued to decline, averaging 1.30 in 1919,
and 1.28, 1.25, 1.24, and 1.22 in the remaining four years. As
with the trend in interlocking, the main declines in density
occur between 1912 and 1935, while the density generally
stabilizes after 1935. Furthermore, this trend appears in both
the full and strong tie networks. Overall, then, the changes in

TABLE 5.3   Network Density

Graph	1904	1912	1919	1935	1964	1969	1974
Full Network							
number of points	166	167	167	167	167	167	167
possible lines	13695	13861	13861	13861	13861	13861	13861
actual lines	983	1050	780	550	610	653	580
density (in %)	7.2	7.6	5.6	4.0	4.4	4.7	4.2
Full Network (connected points only)							
number of points	154	140	143	145	153	153	145
possible lines	11781	9730	10153	10440	11628	11628	10440
actual lines	983	1050	780	550	610	653	580
density (in %)	8.3	10.8	7.7	5.3	5.2	5.6	5.6
Strong Tie Network							
number of points	166	167	167	167	167	167	167
possible lines	13695	13861	13861	13861	13861	13861	13861
actual lines	403	389	309	225	233	256	209
density (in %)	2.9	2.8	2.2	1.6	1.7	1.8	1.5

(Continued)

TABLE 5.3 Continued

Graph	1904	1912	1919	1935	1964	1969	1974
Strong Tie Network (connected points only)							
number of points	128	130	134	130	144	145	135
possible lines	8128	8385	8911	8385	10296	10440	9045
actual lines	403	389	309	225	233	256	209
density (in %)	5.0	4.6	3.5	2.7	2.3	2.5	2.3
% of strong ties/all ties	41.0	37.0	39.6	40.9	38.2	39.2	36.0
interlocks/links	1.557	1.441	1.300	1.284	1.246	1.242	1.217

TABLE 5.4   Interlocked Position Ratio

	1904	1912	1919	1935	1964	1969	1974
Total Number board positions	2595	2761	2834	2819	3350	3511	3282
Interlocked positions	998	974	914	784	929	987	890
IPR (in %)	38.5	35.3	32.3	27.8	27.7	28.1	27.1

network density follow those of interlocking almost identically. Substantial declines took place from 1912 to 1935. After 1935, density eased slightly upward in the full network, and slightly downward in the strong tie network. But these changes do not appear significant. Hence, as with Hypothesis 1, Hypothesis 2 is supported from 1912 through 1935, but is not supported from 1935 to 1974.

The interlocked position ratio (IPR) follows a similar pattern, as indicated in Table 5.4. The IPR declined steadily from 1904 to 1935, and then stabilized. This, again, supports the managerialist position up to 1935, but not thereafter. However, another point of note is that the average number of board positions among the 167 corporations jumped from 16.9 per corporation in 1935 to 20.1 in 1964 and 21.0 in 1969. The increase in board size is a result of several factors. One reason is undoubtedly the increased complexity of corporate bureaucracies, which makes it necessary for companies to have knowledgeable officers on the board. The fact that nearly three-quarters of the newly added directorships involve noninterlocked directors supports this argument. At the same time, the fact that the number of interlocked positions rises to early 1900s levels (especially in 1969), even given the decline in interlocks within the system, suggests a significant decline of multiple interlocking by individuals. And indeed, from 24 individuals with 6 or more board positions in 1904 and 27 in 1912, there was a drop to 14 in 1919, 3 in 1935, 4 in 1964, 2 in 1969, and none in 1974. This adds substance to the claim that there has been a decline in the importance of a few specific individuals within the corporate world, and that institutional relationships have increased in importance (see Chapter 7).

Despite similar declines in both the density and the IPR, the reach of the network does not change appreciably. The results of the reach calculation are presented in Table 5.5, with reach percentages presented for the major clusters and for the entire network. In all seven years, there was one large, completely connected component (cluster) encompassing the vast majority of firms in the system. Within the large clusters, only two corporations are ever as far as five steps from the center. In all seven years, over 95 percent of the corporations are three or fewer steps from the center. Since the one-step reach depends solely on the number of direct ties to the most central corporation, the best basis for comparison appears to be the two-step reach. And since the number of corporations within the large clusters varies among the different years, the most standard way to measure the reach is to include all corporations in the network.

From 1912 to 1935, the decline in reach corresponded with declines in density and IPR, with two-step reach hitting a low

TABLE 5.5   Percentage of Corporations Reached from Most Central Point

Number of Steps	1904	1912	1919	1935	1964	1969	1974
			Major Component				
One	28.8	32.3	20.4	16.5	19.1	25.0	16.0
Two	83.0	91.2	81.7	66.9	75.7	82.9	70.1
Three	98.0	100.0	100.0	96.4	98.7	99.3	97.9
Four	100.0	100.0	100.0	99.3	100.0	100.0	99.3
			Total Network				
One	26.7	26.7	17.5	13.9	17.5	22.9	13.9
Two	77.0	74.7	69.9	56.0	69.3	75.9	60.8
Three	90.9	81.9	85.5	80.7	90.4	91.0	84.9
Four	92.7	81.9	85.5	83.1	91.6	91.6	86.1

point of 56 percent in 1935. However, after 1935, the reach increased to the 1919 level (in 1964) and to the pre-1919 level in 1969. Then, in 1974, it again dropped considerably.

Several points are of note. First, in all seven periods the reach is extensive. In every year under study, over 80 percent of the corporations in the total network are three or fewer steps from the center. Second, the reach hits its low point in 1935, the year of lowest interlocking and lowest total density. Since the recent levels are virtually as high as at the turn of the century, the network can be considered as connected today as in earlier decades, if not as tightly connected (dense). This finding not only fails to support the managerialist hypothesis, but in fact suggests almost the opposite. The rapidity with which information can be communicated is as high in 1964 and 1969 as in 1904 and 1912. On the other hand, because of the lower density in the later years, there are not as many routes by which the information can spread. This would appear to place the highly central corporations in positions of greater relative influence. This question will be taken up in the following chapter, when the distribution of centrality is discussed.

To conclude the analysis of network connectivity, as with interlocking, both the density and the interlocked position ratio (IPR) declined significantly between 1912 and 1935, but stabilized thereafter. This again suggests that the managerialist claims were accurate during the period up to the Depression, but not for the post-Depression era. The trends in network radius not only fail to support the managerialist argument, but may suggest the opposite, that is, that the connectivity of the network has *increased* since 1935. Despite a decline in the tightness of the network, the distance among the corporations does not increase, and actually decreases after 1935.

Centrality of Various Sectors

Earlier in this chapter, I pointed to the sweeping changes in the centrality of industrials and transports. In this section, the changing centrality of all five sectors is examined. First, all sectors will be considered. Then, attention will focus on financial corporations.

Table 5.1, discussed above, lists the mean number of interlocks by sector for all seven years. In the early years, transports (all railroads at the time) and banks were the most heavily interlocked, while industrials and investment banks were the least interlocked. As we move into the recent years, banks maintain their relatively high number of interlocks, while transports become less and less interlocked. Corresponding almost directly with the decline of transport interlocking is the gradual increase of industrial interlocking after 1935. By 1974, industrial interlocking is nearly twice that of transports, compared to one-half in 1935, and even less in earlier years. Did the pattern of interlocking change significantly during the 1904-1974 period? To determine this, a two-way analysis of variance was performed, with sector and time as the independent variables and number of interlocks as the dependent variable. The results are presented in Table 5.6.[3]

These findings demonstrate a number of things. First, interlocking differs significantly among the different years, a finding also reported above. Second, the differences in interlocking among sectors are far more significant than the differences over time, accounting for 16.0 percent of the total variation in

TABLE 5.6   Interlocks by Sector Over Time (Log + 1 Transformation)

	Source of Variance	F value	d.f.	p	% total SS accounted for
A.	Year	5.282	6	.001*	2.1
B.	Sector	61.905	4	.001*	16.0
C.	Interaction (A × B)	5.536	24	.001*	8.6
	Explained (A + B + C)	12.126	34	.001*	26.7

* significant

TABLE 5.7   Centrality by Sector Over Time (Log + 1 Transformation)

	Source of Variance	F value	d.f.	p	% total SS accounted for
A.	Year	9.901	6	.001*	4.3
B.	Sector	13.439	4	.001*	3.9
C.	Interaction (A × B)	5.043	24	.001*	8.9
	Explained (A + B + C)	6.888	34	.001*	17.1

* significant

interlocking. And third, there is a significant alteration in the relative interlocking among sectors over time, as indicated by the interaction effect (8.5 percent).

A two-way analysis of variance on centrality scores using the strong tie directional criteria was also performed. The results of this analysis are presented in Table 5.7.[4] Although the directional criteria still produce significant main effects and interactions, there are considerable differences between the two measures. Overall, the effects on centrality are not as strong. For the year differences we might not expect differences in system centrality over time, since, unlike absolute interlocking, centrality scores are always standardized to between 0 and 1.[5] But the independent effect of the sectors is much lower on directional centrality (3.9 percent) than on interlocking (16.0 percent). And yet the year-sector interaction, the crucial point here, is slightly stronger on centrality (8.9 percent to 8.6 percent on interlocking).

To understand the implications of these findings, we need to discover the sources of the significant effects, that is, which years and which sectors account for the most variation in centrality. We have already seen that the 1912-1935 period accounts for most of the variation related purely to time. But what of the other two effects? The first step in examining this is to compare the changes in centrality over time for each individual sector. Table 5.8 presents a comparison of the mean central-

TABLE 5.8   Centrality by Year for Each Sector (Log + 1 Trans-
             formation)

Sector	F	d.f.	p	% total SS accounted for
Industrials	17.919	6 & 692	.000*	13.4
Transports	2.663	6 & 168	.017*	8.7
Insurances	3.070	6 & 63	.011*	22.6
Investment Banks	3.555	6 & 77	.004*	21.7
Banks	2.016	6 & 133	.067	8.3

* significant at .05.

ity over time for each sector. The table demonstrates that there
were significant changes in centrality in four of the five sectors.
Only changes in bank centrality were not significant at the .05
level. Table 5.9 lists the deviations from the total sector mean in
each year for each sector. These results indicate that industrial
and insurance company centrality increased over time, while
that of transports and investment banks declined. Bank centrality, despite significant increases in 1935 and 1969, remained
basically stable.

Hence, given (1) the significant changes in centrality among
the sectors over time; (2) the significant differences among the
sectors within each year (except 1964); and (3) significant
interaction effects of sector and year, there is no doubt that
there have been major changes in the relative importance of the
various sectors over the past 75 years. We now turn to an
analysis of the specific sectors.

TRANSPORTATION

Table 5.10 presents a comparison of the centrality of the five
sectors for all seven years. The most consistent changes have
occurred between the industrial and transportation sectors. In
the early part of the century, transports were highly central (as
well as heavily interlocked). Although their mean centrality was
far less than that of banks (.134 versus .257), they become

TABLE 5.9 Centrality by Year for Each Sector: Deviations from the Sector Means (Log + 1 Transformation)

Sector	1904	1912	1919	1935	1964	1969	1974	Total Sector Mean
Industrials	- .27	- .66	- .32	- .34	+ .19	+ .79	+ .51	1.90
Transports	+ .44	+ .27	+ .09	+ .25	- .19	- .29	- .59	2.22
Insurances	- .18	-1.13	- .54	+ .16	+ .37	+ .87	+ .43	2.19
Investment Banks	+ .77	+ .55	+ .65	- .10	- .28	- .42	-1.15	1.92
Banks	- .05	- .11	- .46	+ .14	- .27	+ .53	+ .23	2.65

113

more central when the log transformation is applied. The reason for this is that there were a few extremely important banks, but also several relatively isolated ones, including three total isolates. This contributed to the high standard deviation for banks (.247), which lowered their importance as logs were applied. There is no doubt that railroads were highly significant at the turn of the century. On the other hand, as we saw in Chapter 3, most of the major railroads were believed to have been controlled by banks and investment banks. Then what accounts for the high railroad centrality in the directional log matrix?

There appear to be two main reasons for this centrality. First, it was investment banks even more than commercial banks which were particularly powerful in 1904 (Brandeis, 1914). J. P. Morgan & Co., the most powerful and central firm of all, was an investment bank, as was Kuhn, Loeb & Co. And investment banks as a whole were more central than railroads. Second, and this applies to the remaining investment banks as well as to the commercial banks, it was evidently only a small group of financial corporations that exercised great power during this period. Despite the clear importance of such banks as First National Bank, National City Bank, U.S. Trust, Title Guarantee & Trust, and Central Trust, there were several relatively isolated banks in our sample. Thus, among the 20 most central corporations in 1904 were 6 commercial banks and 4 investment banks, but only 5 railroads, only 1 of which was among the top 12 (compared with 8 banks). On the other hand, there was only 1 railroad isolate, and the log standard deviation among the railroads was only .93, compared with 1.28 for banks. This would seem to indicate that, unlike the situation with banks, the great majority of railroads were significant members of the network.

Despite the high centrality of transports in 1904, we can witness a significant and consistent decline during the 70-year period up to 1974. Only between 1919 and 1935 did transport centrality increase. However, after 1935 it dropped considerably and the standard deviation generally increased, reflecting a growing number of isolates. This decrease in centrality appears

TABLE 5.10   Centrality by Sector for Each Year (Log + 1
               Transformation)

	Mean Centrality	SD	% total SS accounted for	% exp. SS accounted for
1904				
Industrials	1.63	1.21	5.1	37.0
Transports	2.66	0.93	4.0	29.0
Insurances	2.01	1.56	0.0	0.0
Investment Banks	2.69	1.18	2.1	15.2
Banks	2.60	1.30	2.7	19.6
Total	2.00	1.28	13.8	*
1912				
Industrials	1.34	1.16	5.7	26.8
Transports	2.49	0.62	5.8	27.2
Insurances	1.06	1.44	1.7	8.0
Investment Banks	2.47	1.02	2.7	12.7
Banks	2.54	1.11	5.4	25.4
Total	1.72	1.23	21.3	*
1919				
Industrials	1.58	1.22	2.9	30.9
Transports	2.31	0.75	2.5	26.6
Insurances	1.65	1.31	0.2	2.1
Investment Banks	2.57	0.78	2.8	29.8
Banks	2.19	1.11	1.1	11.7
Total	1.84	1.16	9.4	*
1935				
Industrials	1.56	1.27	4.5	32.8
Transports	2.47	1.09	2.9	21.2
Insurances	2.35	1.31	0.7	5.1
Investment Banks	1.82	1.41	0.0	0.2
Banks	2.80	0.83	5.7	41.6
Total	1.91	1.29	13.7	*
1964				
Industrials	2.09	1.28	0.0	0.0
Transports	2.03	1.39	0.1	4.2
Insurances	2.56	0.67	0.8	33.3
Investment Banks	1.64	1.31	1.0	41.7
Banks	2.38	1.31	0.5	20.8
Total	2.11	1.27	2.4	(not significant)

(Continued)

TABLE 5.10   Continued

	Mean Centrality	SD	% total SS accounted for	% exp. SS accounted for
1969				
Industrials	2.70	1.00	0.7	4.3
Transports	1.93	1.35	4.7	29.0
Insurances	3.06	0.64	1.1	6.8
Investment Banks	1.50	1.65	6.4	39.5
Banks	3.18	0.57	3.3	20.4
Total	2.57	1.14	16.2	
1974				
Industrials	2.41	1.18	1.0	5.9
Transports	1.63	1.44	3.3	19.5
Insurances	2.62	1.19	0.5	3.0
Investment Banks	0.77	1.41	9.3	55.0
Banks	2.88	0.76	2.8	16.6
Total	2.24	1.30	16.9	

* In some cases the total did not equal 100% due to rounding error.

to reflect the decline of the railroads in the United States after World War II. The most significant decline occurred between 1935 and 1964, paralleling the growth of suburbanization and greater use of automobiles and trucks for transportation. It must be added that by 1964 transports included not only railroads but airlines as well (5 in all). By 1969, the 25 largest transportation firms included 9 airlines as well as 1 bus company (Greyhound) and 1 shipping company. By 1974, 10 airlines and 2 trucking firms were included. How do the nonrailroads compare with the rails during these three years? We might expect the new forms of transportation to be more central as a result of their increasing importance relative to railroads. Table 5.11 provides a comparison based on both the number of interlocks and directional centrality.

There does not appear to be a clear pattern here. Although the mean nonrail centrality declined significantly relative to railroad centrality during this period, the major reason appears to be the increased number of nonrailroad corporations in the

TABLE 5.11   Characteristics of Transportation Industries, 1964-1974

Year	Number of RRs	Number of non-RRs	Mean Number of Interlocks RRs	non-RRs	Mean Centrality (dir., logs) RRs	non-RRs
1964	20	5	8.1	9.8	1.92	2.47
1969	13	11	8.1	5.4	2.04	1.79
1974	13	12	5.8	3.8	1.87	1.37

sample. If we compare only the five largest (in size) nonrails over this time period, there is essentially no difference between them and railroads. The five largest airlines average 9.8, 9.2, and 6.0 interlocks during the three years, compared with 8.1, 8.1, and 5.8 for all railroads. Thus, regardless of whether we consider railroads or airlines, the transportation industry is simply not as centrally located in the American corporate structure as it was prior to World War II. The massive trend toward suburbanization and the use of private means of transportation would seem to be a major reason for this phenomenon.

INDUSTRIALS

The declining centrality of transports during this century has been accompanied by a steady growth in the centrality of industrial corporations. Tables 5.8, 5.9, and 5.10 demonstrate the growing importance of industrials. Industrial centrality has undergone significant changes over time ($F = 17.919$ w. 6 & 692 d.f., $p < .0001$), with 13.4 percent of the variation accounted for by the year intervals, and nearly all of the changes have been in the direction of increased centrality. The most significant increases occurred between 1912 and 1919, and especially from 1935 through 1969. While transports moved from significant positive variance to significant negative variance, industrials did the opposite, although even in recent years industrials do not account for as much positive variance as transports did in the early 1900s.

The widespread changes in the American economy during the twentieth century can be viewed at a glance by looking at the different types of corporations represented. In the early 1900s, there was a preponderance of railroad-related industries, such as coal and railroad car producers. In 1912, 12 of the 100 largest industrials were directly owned by or related to railroads. These included railroad parts suppliers, such as Pullman Co. and Pressed Steel Car, as well as companies such as Great Northern Iron Ore Properties and Lehigh Valley Coal, the latter two owned directly by the parent railroads. By 1964, only 1 of the largest 100 industrials (General American Transportation) could be similarly classified. Meanwhile, recent years have witnessed a growth in the aircraft, chemical, and data processing industries.

But in order to examine the extent to which the significance of an industry is reflected in its network centrality, it is necessary to analyze an industry which was well represented in all seven years. The best candidate for this comparison is the petroleum refining industry. In 1904 only 4 oil companies were included among the 99 largest industrials. However, by 1912, after the court-ordered dissolution of the Standard Oil Trust, 15 companies were represented. In each year from 1912 through 1974, between 15 and 21 oil companies were among the top 100 industrials. The significance of the oil industry should parallel that of the automobile industry and should increase as the coal industry and rail transportation become less important. Thus, the hypothesis here is that if network centrality is a valid indicator of the importance of a company (or industry) in the economy and a measure of the importance of control over specific resources, then *the mean centrality of oil companies should increase over time.*

One problem with directly examining this hypothesis is that we already know that industrial centrality as a whole increased during this period. Unless we are able to specify which industries should become more central and under what circumstances, we run the risk of post hoc explanation. Therefore, to examine this hypothesis I shall treat not only oil companies per se but also how they relate to industrials as a whole.

TABLE 5.12   Mean Centrality: Petroleum Refiners Versus All Industrials
(Log + 1 Transformation)

	1912	1919	1935	1964	1969	1974
Oil Refiners	0.34	0.99	1.22	1.78	2.14	1.96
Non-Oil Industrials	1.52	1.72	1.63	2.17	2.82	2.53
All Industrials	1.34	1.58	1.56	2.09	2.70	2.41

Table 5.12 gives the mean directional centrality (in logs) for petroleum refiners, nonpetroleum industrials, and industrials as a whole, from 1912 to 1974. As the table indicates, oil company centrality increased consistently and often dramatically between 1912 and 1969, then dropped slightly in 1974. This parallels the growing centrality of industrials in general. The oil company increases are generally stronger and more consistent than the non-oil increases. However, oil company centrality is consistently lower than that of non-oil industrials. So, the hypothesis of increasing oil company centrality is supported, but considering that they remain less central than other industrials, one would have to conclude that the support is only moderate.

Which industries are more central? The steel industry, for one. Although steel is of course highly necessary for building automobiles, it was also important for the building of railroad cars. The trend in steel corporation centrality also follows very closely that of industrials as a whole. But steel companies maintain a level slightly higher than the industrial average. Mean steel centrality for the six years (in logs) was 1.65, 1.68, 1.40, 2.41, 2.93, and 2.59, with the number of firms ranging from a high of 11 to a low of 8.

In general, the results on industrial centrality provide some support for the resource dependence model. By looking at the economy in a broad fashion, the transportation and industrial sectors are in network positions commensurate with their importance at various points in the twentieth century. As railroads declined in importance in American society, especially after World War II, railroad network centrality declined significantly. As private means of transportation and housing became more common with the growth of suburbanization, the centrality of oil companies increased, reflecting the growing importance of oil as a resource.

Because it suggests an increase in the influence of nonfinancial corporations, the increasing centrality of industrials would appear to support the managerialist position. However, we have yet to assess the relation between industrials and financial corporations. It is to this latter group that we now turn.

FINANCIAL CORPORATIONS

The fact that financial corporations were highly central in the early part of the century comes as no surprise. Every theoretical perspective, including the managerialist one, agrees that the turn of the century could be considered the "era of finance capital." But, as we have seen, the managerialist position predicts that the dependence of nonfinancials on financials should decrease during the 70-year period under investigation. As mentioned above, financial corporations in this data set include insurance companies and investment banks as well as commercial banks. Thus, the 3 sectors will be treated both separately and as a group. In Chapter 4, 6 hypotheses regarding financials were developed (Hypotheses 5-10). The first of these, that interlocks between financials and nonfinancials would decline, is derived from Allen (1974: 402-403). Table 5.13 gives the breakdown, with each financial sector listed separately.

The pattern in Table 5.13 generally follows that of interlocking as a whole, with the highest levels in the early years, a major decline between 1912 and 1935, and a leveling off thereafter. However, the pattern is not an exact replica of interlocks in general. From 1935 to 1969, financial interlocking with nonfinancials increased considerably, by about 26 percent, before dropping again in 1974. Table 5.14 presents the ratio of financial-nonfinancial interlocking to total interlocking for all seven years.

TABLE 5.13   Interlocks Between Financials and Nonfinancials

Nonfinancial Interlocks with	1904	1912	1919	1935	1964	1969	1974
Insurance Companies	145	83	90	85	112	94	80
Investment Banks	54	58	50	24	32	28	10
Banks	413	532	325	250	271	329	284
All Financials	612	673	465	359	415	451	374

TABLE 5.14   Ratio of Financial-Nonfinancial to Total Interlocks

	1904	1912	1919	1935	1964	1969	1974
A. Financial-Nonfinancial	612	673	465	359	415	451	374
B. All Interlocks	1531	1513	1014	706	760	811	706
A/B (in %)	40.0	44.5	45.9	50.8	54.6	55.6	53.0
Insurance/B (in %)	9.5	5.5	8.9	12.0	14.7	11.6	11.3
Investment Banks/B (in %)	3.5	3.8	4.9	3.4	4.2	3.5	1.4
Bank/B (in %)	27.0	35.2	32.1	35.4	35.7	40.6	40.2

Nonfinancial interlocking with investment banks remained generally stable over time, with two exceptions. First, from 1919 to 1935 there was a major decline in the proportion of investment bank-nonfinancial interlocking among all interlocks (4.9 percent to 3.4 percent). Second, from 1969 to 1974 there was a significant decline in investment bank interlocking. The other two financial sectors, insurance companies and banks, showed consistent increases in interlocks with nonfinancials as a proportion of total interlocks within the system. In short, while the absolute number of financial-nonfinancial (F-NF) interlocks is not as high in recent years as in the 1904-1912 period, it is higher in recent years than in its low point of 1935. Furthermore, the proportion of F-NF interlocks within the system has increased during the century, from a low of 40.0 percent in

1904 to a high of 55.6 percent in 1969. While some of this may be attributable to the heavy interlocking between banks in 1904 and 1912 (prior to the Clayton Act), the 1919 figure of 45.9 percent was only slightly higher than the 44.5 percent in 1912. The sharpest increases occurred during the period prior to the Depression (1919-1935) and from 1935 to 1964. Hence, these data indicate a growing relative importance of financial corporations (in particular banks and insurance companies) in the corporate network. This is the opposite of what the managerialist perspective would expect, and similar to what Allen (1974) found in his 1935-1970 comparison.

Centrality of financial corporations. As pointed out in Chapter 4, the managerialist thesis would expect a decline of financial centrality over time. The results of this hypothesis can be found in Tables 5.8 through 5.10. The centrality of all three financial sectors changes significantly over time (Table 5.8), although for banks the figure is not significant at the .05 level (p = .067). The analysis of variance in Table 5.10 allows us to compare the sectoral centrality in relation to the network as a whole.

Insurance company centrality was about average in 1904, but then dropped off in 1912. This was probably a result of the Armstrong Investigation of 1905, in which insurance companies were forced to divest themselves of a number of holdings in other corporations. Beginning in 1919 insurance company centrality began to increase, exceeding the mean in 1935 and reaching a peak in 1969 (though still accounting for only 1.1 percent of the variance in centrality). The precise role of insurance companies in the economy has been a matter of considerable confusion over the years. As Mariolis (1975) points out, some theorists see insurance companies as the equals of banks, others see them as sometimes equal and sometimes not, and others simply ignore them. Two things are apparent: (1) the largest insurance companies are regular members of major loan consortia (Kotz, 1978); and (2) insurance companies tend to be long-term lenders, while banks specialize in short-term loans. There has been little systematic study of the role of insurance companies in the corporate network, and a comprehensive analysis is beyond the scope of this study. Nevertheless, from the data presented here, it is clear that since 1912 insurance companies have taken on an increasingly important role within the American economy.

Investment banks (IBs), on the other hand, have undergone a decline in centrality. The early 1900s are often considered the heyday of investment banking, typified in the person of J. P. Morgan. During this period, the investment banks held sway over the capital needed by the nearly bankrupt railroads and the newly emerging industrial giants, and they were prominent in the merging together of "trusts" such as U.S. Steel and International Harvester. This was reflected in the high centrality of investment banks from 1904 through 1919. But in 1935, the IB centrality dropped off considerably, to about the network mean. By 1964 it had fallen significantly below the network mean, to a point at which, by 1974, IBs accounted for 55.0 percent of the variation explained by type of corporation (because of their low centrality). Thus, investment banks, while not unimportant, are not nearly as significant as they once were.[6]

This "decline of the investment banker" has been cited by many theorists as the harbinger of managerialism (see Sweezy, 1941; Bell, 1960). What is often ignored by these writers is the reason for the decline, as well as the continuing importance of commercial banks. Responding to public pressure during the 1930s, the Glass-Steagull Act of 1933 required the separation of investment and commercial banking. Prior to this time, many of the major banks engaged in both activities. After Glass-Steagull, J. P. Morgan & Co. became strictly a commercial bank, and a group of Morgan partners formed the separate investment house of Morgan, Stanley, & Co. The remaining investment banks were forced to give up their deposits, which had been a major source of bank capital. By doing so, investment banks became dependent on commercial banks for financing, further lowering their power (Kotz, 1978). Thus, the focus of financial activity shifted to the commercial banking sector. Investment banks have since participated mainly in the legal aspects of corporate activity such as underwriting stock issues and corporate mergers. They continue to perform an important function and they are not without influence, but compared with their position at the turn of the twentieth century, the power of investment banks has declined considerably.

Commercial banking, on the other hand, is the only sector whose centrality is above average for all seven years. Banks reached their highest relative centrality (in percentage of variance accounted for) at three points: 1912, 1935, and 1969. Their lowest points were in 1919 and 1964. Thus, bank centrality does not follow an overall trend. Banks were highly central early in the century and remained that way throughout the 70-year period.

This finding is remarkable in certain respects. First, while 1912 can be viewed as the high point of the finance capital period, much of the high bank centrality was attributable to the heavy interlocking among banks ("horizontal" interlocking), which was subsequently outlawed in 1914. In 1912 there were 124 interlocks between banks. By 1919 there were only 19. And, corresponding with this, the percentage of variance in centrality accounted for by banks declined from 5.4 percent in 1912 to 1.1 percent in 1919. But by 1935, even with the restrictions against horizontal interlocking, banks accounted for 5.7 percent of the variation in centrality.

The high bank centrality in both 1935 and 1969 corresponded with significant economic events: 1935 was the middle of the Great Depression. Banks could be expected to be important in times of crisis (Mintz and Schwartz, 1980). As corporations become less profitable or go into bankruptcy, creditors want to be in a position to monitor the policies of their clients. When the Erie Railroad went into receivership in 1893, it was J. P. Morgan who presided over the reorganization. The period of the late 1960s was characterized by an unprecedented wave of mergers in the American economy. Banks encourage the rise of conglomerates because it leads to a decrease in competition, thereby providing a safer environment for investment (Kotz,

1979). Thus, banks are often instrumental in directing merger activity. Two quantitative analyses have found supportive evidence for the idea that interlocks increase as companies experience difficulty. Pfeffer (1972) found that bank representation on a firm's board was significantly related to the corporation's debt-equity ratio. And Bunting (1976a) found a curvilinear relationship between interlocks and profitability. Up to a point, profitability increased as interlocks increased. However, the most interlocked corporations were on the whole less profitable than average. Whether interlocking typically increases among firms in crisis situations is an important area for further research.

To recap, the managerialist hypothesis of declining bank centrality over time is not supported by the data. Bank centrality has remained high during the entire period, peaking at specific points, but revealing no consistent pattern of change.

The above hypotheses dealt with all corporations in the particular sectors. Hence, they ignored the effect that a few particularly central or isolated corporations might have on the means for the entire sector. However, we are interested not only in whole sectors but also in the centrality of particular corporations. In Chapter 3 it was shown that in 1904, 12 of the 20 most central corporations in the directional network were financial corporations (60 percent) although only 25 percent of the firms in the network were financials. As I pointed out, these highly central corporations were among the most powerful in the economy at the time. The managerialist thesis predicts that over time, the number of financials among the most central corporations will decline.

Table 5.15 presents a comparison of the percentage of financials among the top 25 and the top 50 for each year. Although in all but one case, the observed frequency of financials among the most central corporations is greater than the expected frequency, the difference is greatest in the 1904-1912 period. After a dip in 1919, 1935 and 1969 were relatively high in terms of financial presence in the center of the network. This corresponds with the earlier findings on overall bank centrality, in which 1904-1912, 1935, and 1969 were the years of highest

TABLE 5.15   Proportion of Financials Among Most Central Corporations

Financials	1904	1912	1919	1935	1964	1969	1974
Among 25 Most Central	14	17	8	12	9	11	7
Percentage	56.0	68.0	32.0	48.0	36.0	44.0	28.0
Among 50 Most Central	23	20	15	21	12	17	15
Percentage	46.0	40.0	30.0	42.0	24.0	34.0	30.0
Percentage Financials in System	25.3	25.1	25.1	25.1	25.1	25.1	25.1

TABLE 5.16   Presence of Financials Among Most Central Corporations (by sector)

	1904	1912	1919	1935	1964	1969	1974
Among 25 Most Central							
Insurance Companies	2	1	1	2	2	3	3
Investment Banks	4	4	3	3	1	2	1
Banks	8	12	4	7	6	6	3
Among 50 Most Central							
Insurance Companies	4	1	2	6	3	5	4
Investment Banks	7	7	5	3	1	3	2
Banks	12	12	8	12	8	9	9

financial centrality. Table 5.16 compares the various financial sectors in the top 25 and the top 50.

These results suggest two things. First, the presence of banks among the top 25 has declined from its 1904-1912 highs, but has generally increased from its 1919 low point. Second, the presence of banks among the top 50 has remained quite stable during the entire period. The presence of investment banks has declined (as in the earlier findings) while that of insurance companies has increased. Overall, then, the main source of the decline of financials among the most central corporations is the descent of investment banks. Furthermore, although bank dominance was highest in the 1904-1912 period, the changes did not conform to the pattern that the managerialist thesis predicts. Rather, from 1919 to 1974, bank representation was fairly stable within both the top 25 and especially the top 50. And finally, the presence of insurance companies actually increases over time, corresponding closely with the decline of investment banks. From these results, it is difficult to argue that financial corporations have declined in importance during the twentieth century.

The next hypothesis deals with the proportion of sending interlocks among financials. If financial corporations have declined in influence over nonfinancials, we should expect fewer of their interlocks to involve sending representatives to other corporations. We can examine this hypothesis for insurance companies and banks. It does not apply to investment banks, since, with a few exceptions, all investment bank interlocks are sending interlocks. However, it should be remembered that investment bank interlocks have declined considerably over time. Table 5.17 presents a comparison of sending and receiving interlocks over time for both insurance companies and banks.

As the table indicates, the proportion of directional interlocks from financials to nonfinancials has declined since 1912. This has occurred fairly consistently for both banks and insurance companies, although insurance companies began to send more from 1964 to 1974. The most significant decline in sending interlocks took place between 1935 and 1964, commensurate with the growing centrality of industrials. This finding supports the managerialist argument that financial dominance over nonfinancials has declined over time. Nevertheless, since there are several ways to interpret this phenomenon, I shall discuss some of the implications of the trend.

The most straightforward interpretation of directional interlocking (and the view argued for in Chapter 2) is to assume a

TABLE 5.17   Financial Directional Interlocks with Nonfinancials

Sector	1904	1912	1919	1935	1964	1969	1974
Insurance Companies							
Sending	26	29	29	16	6	11	13
Receiving	22	11	10	10	18	22	10
% Sending	54.2	72.5	74.4	61.5	25.0	33.3	56.5
Banks							
Sending	57	103	79	59	58	64	49
Receiving	66	74	61	43	67	75	74
% Sending	46.3	58.2	56.4	57.8	46.4	46.0	39.8
% Sending (insurance companies + banks)	48.5	60.8	60.3	58.6	45.6	43.6	42.5
% Sending (all financials)	60.1	65.2	68.1	64.3	52.2	51.0	46.2

direct relationship between sending and influence. For example, J. P. Morgan solidified his control over U.S. Steel by placing three J. P. Morgan & Co. representatives on the U.S. Steel board. Thus, when in 1969 we have a representative of IBM on the board of Morgan Guaranty Trust, this presumably indicates a certain amount of IBM influence over Morgan. Since there are more and more cases of the latter over time, the logical conclusion is that nonfinancial corporations are assuming more power over financials, or at least that relations are becoming less one-sided. This view is consistent with the managerialist thesis, and it has empirical support in our data.

Ironically, the cooptation model would lead one to the exact opposite conclusion. Since in this view the receiving (coopting) organization is the more powerful one, then the trend toward more financial receiving interlocks would indicate an increasing ability of financial corporations to absorb potentially disruptive elements in their environments. Our historical evidence leads to the conclusion that the cooptation view has little foundation when analyzing directional interlocking early in the twentieth century. Thus, the only way that the cooptation model can be salvaged is to argue that the meaning of directional interlocking has changed during the course of the century. But, even if this argument is made, cooptation theorists would be forced to concede that the power of financials has remained at the very least constant over time.

In the absence of evidence to the contrary, the only consistent strategy is to continue to treat sending interlocks as indicators of influence. As I argued in Chapter 2, there is nothing in this view which is inconsistent with the idea that control over crucial resources is a basis for power in interorganizational relations. But it is *not* consistent with the cooptation model, in which interlocking is seen as an essentially defensive strategy. For this reason, as indicated above, I refer to the influence view presented in this study as a "modified" resource dependence model.

Given the increasing proportion of receiving interlocks, have bank boards become meeting places for members of a particular industry who cannot legally interlock, as governmental and legal critics of interlocking have feared? Bunting (1976b), for example, found that indirect interlocking by members of a particular industry through bank boards increased significantly between 1964 and 1974, from 108 in 1964 to 164 in 1974. However, he counted all indirect interlocks without regard to direction. If industry members were in fact using banks specifically for the purpose of creating indirect interlocks, we would expect the number of industry officers meeting on bank boards to increase as well. An examination of this process from 1904 to 1974 suggests that this situation is relatively rare. The number of indirect officer ties by members of the same industry is presented in Table 5.18. The table is broken down by three categories of *Dun and Bradstreet's* "Standard Industrial Classifications." Each successive digit indicates increasing industry similarity. Comparisons between industrial and transportation sectors are also presented.

The table indicates that while 1904 and 1912 were the years of greatest indirect interlocking, virtually all of this was ac-

TABLE 5.18   Indirect Horizontal Officer Links Through Banks by Members of the Same Industry

SIC Classification	1904	1912	1919	1935	1964	1969	1974
Two-Digit (major group)	1	2	3	0	4	6	6
Three-Digit (industry subgroup)	0	0	2	0	0	0	0
Four-Digit (detailed industry)	20	14	8	3	6	7	4
Industrial Links	5	2	9	0	10	13	10
Transport Links	16	14	4	3	0	0	0
Total	21	16	13	3	10	13	10

counted for by railroads. After 1912, except for 1935, in which essentially no such interlocking occurred, nearly all indirect interlocking was by industrials. In the 1964-1974 period, all indirect officer interlocks were within the industrial sector. Another interesting point is that, while up to 1935 only 1 of the 8 4-digit industrial links was between oil companies, from 1964-1974 12 of the 17 ties were between oil companies. Compared with the actual number of direct interlocks, the number of ties accomplished by officers of firms in the same industry is quite small. Furthermore, when all such ties are counted, the number in recent years is considerably less than in the 1904-1912 period, when direct within-industry interlocking was legal. Nevertheless, if we treat only industrials, the frequency of indirect officer interlocking has increased significantly since 1912, particularly since 1935. This suggests that among industrials, this practice may indeed become increasingly prevalent in the future.

Other theorists, in particular Sweezy (1972) and Domhoff (1979), have argued that it no longer makes sense to separate finance capital from industrial capital, that instead the two interests have effectively merged.[7] The apparent decline of direct financial control signified by the decline in financial sending interlocks would seem to support this argument. Nevertheless, financial centrality in the directional network relative to that in the full and strong tie networks does *not* decline over time, as the managerialist thesis would predict. Table 5.19 presents the ratios of mean centrality to the grand mean (in logs) for all seven years for each of the three financial sectors. As the table indicates, there is not a systematic pattern for banks over time (insurance companies become relatively more central in the directional network). As with the previous measures, 1912 and 1935 appear as peak years for banks. However, 1969 does not stand out in a similar manner. In fact, for every year except 1964, relative directional centrality for banks is higher than their relative full or strong tie centrality. Even with the increase in the proportion of bank receiving interlocks, banks remain more central in the directional network than they do in the two nondirectional ones.

The final hypothesis about financial corporations concerns the relative "stability" of the most central corporations over time. According to the finance capital perspective, the major financials should remain highly central over time, while the high centrality of a particular nonfinancial is more likely to be a temporary phenomenon. If the managerialist thesis is accurate, we should witness successively less financial stability relative to nonfinancials over time. If we take managerialism a step further, we should see less and less stability of any type in more recent years. To examine this hypothesis, the 25 most central corporations from each year were compared with those of the next closest year of data. The results are tabulated by financials versus nonfinancials and are presented in Table 5.20.

In terms of continuity from one year to the next, financial corporations tend to be more stable than nonfinancials. While the 86 percent financial continuity between 1904 and 1912 is not subsequently approached, only once does nonfinancial continuity exceed 50 percent (1912-1919), and it goes as low as 8 percent from 1935 to 1964. Of the 13 nonfinancial corporations among the 25 most central in 1935, only 1 was among the top 25 in 1964. Interestingly, it was precisely this period during

TABLE 5.19   Relation of Mean Financial Centrality to Grand Mean
              (Log + 1 Transformation)

Sector	1904	1912	1919	1935	1964	1969	1974
Insurance Companies							
Full Network	1.00	.82	1.00	1.26	1.19	1.16	1.14
Strong Tie Network	.95	.63	.93	1.22	1.32	1.22	1.27
Directional Network	1.00	.62	.90	1.23	1.21	1.19	1.17
Investment Banks							
Full Network	.94	1.01	1.06	.70	.67	.42	.23
Strong Tie Network	1.19	1.23	1.25	.77	.69	.49	.28
Directional Network	1.35	1.43	1.39	.95	.78	.58	.34
Banks							
Full Network	1.23	1.31	1.17	1.29	1.14	1.18	1.22
Strong Tie Network	1.24	1.44	1.16	1.49	1.14	1.21	1.31
Directional Network	1.30	1.48	1.19	1.46	1.13	1.23	1.28

TABLE 5.20   Continuity and Stability of Most Central Corporations

Interval:	1904-1912		1912-1919		1919-1935		1935-1964		1964-1969		1969-1974	
	F	NF	F	NF	F	NF	F	NF	F	NF	F	NF
S	12	2	7	5	6	6	6	1	6	5	5	7
NS	2	9	10	3	2	11	6	12	3	11	6	7

NOTE: F = financial; NF = nonfinancial; S = among 25 most central firms in both years; NS = among 25 most central firms in the first year but not in the second.

which industrials clearly replaced transports as the most central nonfinancial sector. Financial stability, on the other hand, is under 50 percent only twice, and is never below 40 percent. Meanwhile, it goes as high as 86 percent, 75 percent, and 67 percent on three different occasions.

An examination of the continuity of particular corporations further demonstrates the stability of financial institutions. Table 5.21 lists the 15 corporations which have been among the 25 most central in 3 or more of the 7 years for which we have data. Among the 7 corporations which have made the list 4 or more times, 5 are financials. Of the 15 which have made the list 3 or more times, 8 are financials. In addition, all 3 railroads which made the list 3 times (Great Northern, Illinois Central, and Reading) were not among the most central corporations after 1935. The 5 most often central corporations include the 4 most historically dominant New York banks: J. P. Morgan & Co., First National City Bank, Chase Manhattan Bank, and Bankers Trust.

TABLE 5.21 Corporations Most Often Among 25 Most Central

Name (most recent)	Type	Number of Years
J. P. Morgan & Co.	Bank	7
First National City Bank	Bank	6
Union Pacific	Transport	6
Bankers Trust	Bank	5
Chase Manhattan Bank	Bank	5
Anaconda Copper	Industrial	4
Mutual Life	Insurance	4
Brown Brothers, Harriman & Co.	Investment Bank*	3
Exxon (Standard Oil of NJ)	Industrial	3
Great Northern	Transport	3
Illinois Central	Transport	3
Kuhn, Loeb & Co.	Investment Bank	3
New York Life	Insurance	3
Procter & Gamble	Industrial	3
Reading	Transport	3
United Aircraft	Industrial	3

* Brown Brothers, Harriman & Co. is in fact a private commercial bank, that is, it is completely owned by members of the Harriman family. Because it is the only such institution in this data set, it is classified as an investment bank because of its character as a partnership. The bank does not have a board of directors elected by public stockholders.

If we include the individual banks which later merged into the first three of the above, we gain an even clearer picture of their dominance. The lead bank in the present J. P. Morgan & Co. is Morgan Guaranty Trust, itself based on a merger between the old J. P. Morgan & Co. and Guaranty Trust. J. P. Morgan was the most central corporation in the network in 1904, 1919, and 1935, and was second in 1912 (the two banks merged in 1959). Guaranty Trust was in the top 25 in 1912, 1919, and 1935, ranking ninth in the latter two years. After dropping to twentieth in 1964, Morgan Guaranty rose to third in 1969, and back to first in 1974. First National City Bank (now known as Citibank) was the result of a 1953 merger between the First National Bank and National City Bank. The former was controlled by George F. Baker, a close ally of Morgan, and the bank remained closely allied to J. P. Morgan & Co., at least through 1935 (Sweezy, 1953). The First National Bank was among the most central corporations from 1904 through 1935, ranking no lower than seventh (1904) and ranking first in 1912. The National City Bank, on the other hand, was at the turn of the century controlled by James Stillman, a close ally of John D. Rockefeller and a rival of Morgan interests. However, after the panic of 1907, the Morgan-Rockefeller conflict was called to a halt by a general agreement by both sides to end "destructive competition" (Corey, 1930; Allen, 1935; Sobel, 1965). National City Bank was among the top 25 in 1904, 1912, and 1935.

By the early 1950s, the First National Bank was in decline, partly as a result of the conversion of J. P. Morgan to a commercial bank (Josephson, 1972), and in 1953 it was absorbed by the National City Bank to form the First National City Bank. The third of the four stable banks, Chase Manhattan Bank, is the result of a 1955 merger between the Chase National and the Manhattan Co. banks. Chase National was among the top 25 in 1912, 1919, and 1935, while Manhattan Co. reached the top 25 in 1935. As with Citibank, Chase Manhattan made the top 25 in 1964 and 1969, but not in 1974. But Chase reached no higher than nineteenth (although it was first in the

1964 full network), while Citibank was ranked first in 1969. Chase National is believed to have come under Rockefeller control in 1930 after it merged with the Rockefeller-controlled Equitable Trust (TNEC, 1940; Elias, 1973; Collier and Horowitz, 1976), and Chase Manhattan is generally believed to be under Rockefeller family control at present. Finally, Bankers Trust has been a long-time Morgan ally and is still considered by many to be a member of the J. P. Morgan & Co. sphere of influence (Menshikov, 1969; Kotz, 1978).

Thus, among the five corporations with the longest periods of high centrality are four major banks, all of which have been seen as cornerstones of the Morgan and Rockefeller empires since the early part of the century. These banks may or may not be the foundations of Morgan and Rockefeller family interests. Regardless, it is clear that, at least as *institutions,* these major banks have been and continue to be the dominant forces in the American corporate network.

The 3 other frequently central corporations, Union Pacific, Mutual Life, and Anaconda Copper, are all historically significant. Union Pacific was the foundation of Edward H. Harriman's railroad empire early in the century, and remains one of the nation's 5 largest railroads. It was among the top 25 in every year except 1912. However, Union Pacific's high centrality in recent years appears to be a result of its situation as a "bridge" (Mintz, 1978), that is, it picks up a high percentage of centrality from one particular link. In 1964, Union Pacific gained 54 percent of its centrality from 5 interlocks with Brown Brothers, Harriman & Co. (BBH), 2 sending and 3 receiving. Although in the directional network no more than 1.5 interlocks per tie are counted in the computation of centrality (equivalent to the maximum of 3 in the nondirectional networks), this still amounts to nearly 2 full sending interlocks for Union Pacific. In 1964, 54 percent of Union Pacific's centrality came from its link with BBH. In 1969, 89 percent of its centrality came from an identical link with BBH. And in 1974, 76 percent of its centrality came from an officer exchange with Anaconda (ranked fourth).

This situation points to a problem with the centrality measure which may have exaggerated Union Pacific's influence in recent years: One particular tie with a highly central firm can dramatically increase a corporation's centrality score. Mintz (1978) treated this by removing from the calculation all links with corporations whose centrality scores were 80 percent or more of the original firm's score. When I did this for the 1964-1974 networks, Union Pacific's rank dropped from fifteenth, twentieth, and tenth in the three years to twenty-third, one-hundred-forty-fifth, and fourteenth. Only in 1969 was Union Pacific linked with another firm whose centrality was 80 percent or more of Union Pacific's, which explains the sharp decline in that year. However, the character of the network as a whole was very similar even after this provision was made, suggesting that this phenomenon was relatively rare. Since both Menshikov and Kotz view Union Pacific as controlled by BBH during the 1960s, Union Pacific's high centrality in these years may be more a function of its character as a bridge than of its actual influence.

The two remaining frequently central corporations, Mutual Life and Anaconda Copper, are both historically significant. Mutual Life, still a major insurance company, was a Morgan stronghold in the early part of the century (Youngman, 1907; Moody, 1919; Brandeis, 1914). Mutual was among the top 25 every year from 1904 through 1935, reaching as high as second in 1919, but was not among the most central thereafter. Anaconda Copper is a descendant of the old Amalgamated Copper, a Rockefeller property ranked sixteenth in 1904. Anaconda, the largest copper mining company in the United States, was eighteenth, thirteenth, and fourth in centrality from 1964 through 1974. As of 1974, prior to its acquisition by Arco, it was still thought to have close ties with Chase Manhattan Bank (Zeitlin, 1974).

For all 7 years, there was a total of 49 corporations that were among the 25 most central for 2 or more years. Of these 49, 25 (51.0 percent) were financials. This finding of high financial stability runs counter to the managerialist thesis, and lends support to the finance capital position. When viewed in terms of resource dependence, it suggests that financial institutions have consistently possessed the most important resource (capital). The one financial sector which has lost its access to capital, investment banking, has also become less central in the network.

DISCUSSION OF EVIDENCE
ON FINANCIAL CORPORATIONS

I have examined six hypotheses concerned with changing financial centrality over time. While some of the findings support the managerialist thesis, most do not. For example, although the number of interlocks between financials and nonfinancials declined over time, virtually all of the decline took place between 1912 and 1919. After 1919 there was no clear trend. A similar situation was found for financial presence among the most central corporations. This number declined from 17 in 1912 to 8 in 1919, but then increased to an average of slightly under 10 for the 1935-1974 period. And although the percentage of financial sending interlocks declined over time, the relative directional centrality of financials compared with their full and strong tie centrality did not decline. Even as financial corporations receive a higher proportion of directors from nonfinancials, their relative centrality remains highest in the directional network. In addition, relative to the total number of interlocks in the system, ties between financials and nonfinancials have become significantly more prominent over time, now involving over 50 percent of all interlocks. Finally, the presence of particular financial corporations among the most central remains highly stable over the 70-year period. Over one-half of all corporations that appear among the 25 most central in 2 or more years are financials. Of the 7 firms that have appeared 4 or more times, 5 are financials.

There are interesting trends among the three financial sectors as well. The centrality of investment banks declines considerably, while that of insurance companies increases. But, interestingly, commercial bank centrality remains highly stable, with only the percentage of bank sending interlocks declining significantly. In sum, whatever decline has occurred among financial corporations appears to have been concentrated in the investment banking sector. What appears to have changed among commercial banks is the phenomenon of directly controlling other corporations by placing officers on the boards of nonfinancial corporations. The importance of banks in recent years is more a function of their centrality in the network. Bank influence has become a more general network phenomenon rather than one based on dyadic control relationships between specific pairs of corporations.

Summary

This chapter has examined hypotheses dealing with two of our three areas of focus. We saw that interlocking and density within the system declined considerably between 1912 and 1935, but stabilized thereafter. Thus, the managerialist thesis was partially supported, but only up to 1935. Furthermore, the distance between corporations declined considerably between 1935 and the 1964-1974 period, running directly counter to the managerialist position.

In comparing the relative centrality of various sectors, we saw that while transports were highly central and industrials were relatively isolated early in the century, by the 1960s industrials had become more central than average while transports became successively less central. Among the financial sectors, insurance companies became slightly more central as the century progressed, but remained fairly stable overall. Investment banks, highly central in the earlier years (1904-1919), became less and less central in the post-Depression era. Commercial bank centrality declined from 1912 to 1919 but increased in 1935 and remained high through 1974. Furthermore, relative to other sectors, there was a remarkable continuity of the most central commercial banks over time. Descendants of the most powerful financial institutions at the turn of the century remain, for the most part, highly central today. The one aspect of bank centrality which has declined is the proportion of sending interlocks. But, even with this trend, banks remain more central in the directional network than in the full and strong tie networks. Thus, despite the decline in the influence of investment banks, financial institutions as a whole remain highly central among major American corporations.

To briefly evaluate the results of the managerialist hypotheses at this point, of the ten hypotheses which have been treated, only one supports the managerialist thesis without qualification. Five hypotheses receive partial support, in all cases based on trends between 1912 and 1935. And four hypotheses are completely disconfirmed by the data. A complete summary will be presented in Chapter 7.

NOTES

1. Whether t-tests or analysis of variance with multiple comparison is performed in this case is largely a matter of the specific theoretical question being asked. Since we are concerned both with particular pairs of years and with the direction of change, a one-tailed t-test is the most appropriate statistical technique. Because of the problems with statistical significance created by the use of six comparisons on seven groups of data, the Bonferroni procedure (Nemenyi, 1978) was employed to determine the appropriate significance level. This is done by dividing the desired significance level by the number of tests to be performed, in this case .05/6. Thus, in order to be confident of significance at the .05 level, I have employed the .01 level when examining the t-test results. It should also be noted that, while an analysis of variance yielded significant differences among the seven years, the results of the multiple comparisons varied depending on the criteria employed. Duncan's multiple range test yielded significant 1912-1919 and 1919-1935 differences at the .05 level. Scheffe's test yielded only significant 1912-1919 differences even at the .10 level.

2. At this point a word on the use of statistical tests is necessary. Since the data in this study do not constitute a random sample, the use of significance levels in the conventional sense is not entirely appropriate. I have employed them at certain points as aids in determining the strength of a relationship, or in cases in which the relations among the variables were complex and not easily discernible without them (as in two-way analyses of variance). However, I have operated with the position that

no hypothesis will be supported or rejected purely on the grounds of statistical significance. Thus, the tests should be viewed as heuristic devices, i.e., as practical guides to understanding the relations among variables.

3. Because the within-group variances were highly unequal, transformations to logarithms of base 10 were performed to equalize the variances. The log + 1 transformation described by Li (1964) was employed so that a firm with 0 interlocks is credited with 1, and hence is 0 since $10^0 = 1$. From this point on, all statistical tests will employ logarithms.

4. Since all but one of the centrality scores is less than 1 (which would produce negative logarithms), the scores were multiplied by 10,000 to remove the decimal point. Hence, all logs of centrality scores range from 0 to 4.0 (the log of 10,000).

5. In fact, the mean system centrality may be significant as an indicator of the distribution of centrality within the system. But this topic is not directly relevant here and will be considered in the following chapter.

6. Commercial banks may now be moving further into activities traditionally reserved for investment banks. According to a *New York Times* (January 30, 1978: D1, D6) story, investment bankers are increasingly concerned that commercial banks are moving into the placement of private securities, i.e., selling their securities directly to insurance companies or trust departments instead of through public issues. A major reason for their fear is that commercial banks have used their control of loan capital to coerce business from various nonfinancials. "In instance after instance, the investment bankers charge, they have lost private placement business because banks exerted pressure on corporate customers already dependent upon the commercial banks for basic financing." According to the head of one investment firm, " 'We have no proof.... All we know is that we come in with specific ideas and the next thing we know, some 30-year-old at a bank signs up that company for long-term credit' " (*New York Times*, January 30, 1978: D1).

7. See also O'Connor (1968, 1972), Menshikov (1969), and Herman (1981).

CHAPTER 6

CLIQUES AND THE DISTRIBUTION
OF CENTRALITY

The previous chapter dealt with characteristics of the network as a whole and the relative prominence of corporations in particular sectors. In this chapter, I shall examine five hypotheses derived from the discussion of interest groups and the distribution of interlocking presented in Chapter 4. Implicit in Allen's (1974, 1978) work is the idea that the development of managerial control has led to a more balanced set of relations among large corporations, and less hierarchy in the system as a whole. The more equally power is distributed within the system, the less likely it is that individual firms will be subject to external domination. Although the managerialist position also predicts a decline in the overall amount of interlocking, to the extent that interlocking does exist, it should be more evenly distributed among the corporations.[1]

In order to measure changes in the distribution of interlocking, the proportion of interlocks involving the most and least interlocked corporations was compared. The results are presented in Table 6.1.

By any criteria, the distribution of interlocking among the 167 corporations in the sample is highly unequal in all 7 years. In 1974, the year of lowest inequality, the top 50 percent of the firms were still involved in 80 percent of all interlocks. Nevertheless, we can witness a clear trend away from inequality during the 70-year period. The only exception to this trend is between 1919 and 1935, when inequality increased slightly. But, while in 1904 the least interlocked 50 percent accounted for only 9 percent of all interlocks, by 1974 they accounted for

TABLE 6.1 Size Distribution of Interlocking

Rank in Interlocks	% of All Interlocks						
	1904	1912	1919	1935	1964	1969	1974
Top 5%	23.8	21.6	17.4	19.6	17.3	17.6	16.1
Top 10%	41.5	37.1	30.6	33.5	30.3	29.7	29.1
Top 20%	60.8	58.0	49.7	52.1	47.6	46.2	45.6
Top 40%	85.0	83.0	78.2	78.9	72.6	71.3	70.2
Top 50%	90.9	90.8	87.0	87.6	81.5	80.4	80.1
Bottom 50%	9.1	9.2	13.0	12.4	18.6	19.6	19.9
Bottom 40%	5.1	4.0	6.4	6.5	11.0	12.1	11.9
Bottom 20%	0.9	0.2	0.4	0.8	1.6	1.7	1.2

about 20 percent. The top fifth of corporations accounted for 60.8 percent of all interlocks in 1904, but for only 45.6 percent in 1974. This finding supports the managerialist thesis.

One possible objection to this conclusion might be that in 1904, 2 corporations had 153 and 111 interlocks, while the next closest firm had 88. In contrast, by 1974 no single corporation had more than 35 interlocks and the next 2 had 34 and 30, respectively. The extreme skewness of the distribution in 1904 might have contributed to an unusually high degree of inequality in the system. However, even when these 2 companies are removed from the calculation, the 5 percent most interlocked corporations still account for 21.7 percent of all interlocks, compared with 23.8 percent with the 2 included. Thus, although the presence of the 2 highly interlocked companies adds considerable inequality to the system, the 1904 system is significantly more unequal than the 1974 system even when they are excluded.

As with the previous hypotheses, centrality figures were also employed. Because of the nature of the centrality scores, the inequality in centrality was analyzed differently. First, since all centrality scores must be between 0 and 1, and since the most central corporation automatically receives a score of 1, the scores of the most central corporations provide an initial indication of the hierarchy in the system. The higher the mean centrality, the less hierarchical the system. But it is also necessary to take the standard deviation into account, since the mean can be driven up by a small number of highly central firms. With this in mind, the hierarchy of the system can be measured by taking the ratio of mean centrality to the standard deviation. The higher the figure, the more equal the distribution of centrality. The results of this calculation for all seven years using directional centrality are presented in Table 6.2.

These results, as with those for interlocking, show a general increase in the equality of centrality distribution over time. However, they are not as consistently unidirectional as the interlocking results. Both 1912 and 1919 are more hierarchical than 1904, and 1935 is about equal to 1904. And although the figures for the 1964-1974 period are considerably higher overall than those of the earlier years, the 1969 figure is substantially higher than both 1964 and 1974. Since these figures should be viewed as estimates, the significant finding is the difference between the 1904-1935 and the 1964-1974 periods. It is clear that centrality has become more equally distributed in recent years. Thus, we have some support for the managerialist view that the system has become less concentrated over time.

The Existence of Cliques

We now turn to an examination of cliques in the network. As I pointed out earlier, the prevalent view among observers of this

TABLE 6.2 Distribution of System Centrality

	1904	1912	1919	1935	1964	1969	1974
Mean	.097	.060	.059	.080	.096	.155	.128
Standard Deviation	.178	.140	.128	.151	.141	.189	.192
Mean/SD	.54	.43	.46	.53	.68	.82	.67

phenomenon is that earlier in the century the economy was characterized by a number of "interest groups" based primarily on family and/or financial ties. However, according to some theorists, these groups have in recent years begun to (a) disintegrate and (b) become based more on geographical similarity than on family or financial ties (Sweezy, 1953; Baran and Sweezy, 1966; Dooley, 1969; Allen, 1978). If these theorists are correct, then in recent years interest groups should be fewer in number, smaller in size, and less exclusive than in the past.

When the peak analysis is applied to the full network of all interlocks, a consistent finding emerges: All seven years are characterized by one huge clique containing the great majority of firms in the network. Only once, in 1912, was there another group of interlocked corporations outside the main cluster, in this case a group of three corporations, General Petroleum, Union Oil, and National Lead. The clique sizes for the seven years were 154, 137, 143, 140, 153, 153, and 145, in sum, relatively equal. The peaks in the seven years were the Erie Railroad, First National Bank, Great Northern-Northern Pacific Railroad, Pullman Co., and Chase Manhattan, First National City, and Chemical banks. As with previous studies by Bearden et al. (1975) and Mariolis (1978), the full matrix peak analysis failed to generate any substantively meaningful groupings.

The strong tie and directional peak analyses yielded similar results from 1904 through 1919. In 1904, the analysis generated a 119-member clique led by J. P. Morgan & Co. Also detected were 3 other small cliques averaging 3 members each. Given the available historical evidence, the picture of a single, large, Morgan-dominated group appears to be an accurate reflection of the corporate system around 1904.

There are two views of the situation at the time. The first is that there were two major groups, dominated by J. P. Morgan on the one hand, and by an alliance of John D. and William Rockefeller (Standard Oil), James Stillman (National City Bank), Jacob Schiff (Kuhn, Loeb & Co.), and Edward H. Harriman (Union Pacific) on the other (Pratt, 1904; Keys,

1910; Bullock, 1903; Youngman, 1907). Another view, held most prominently by John Moody (1919), held that, despite the existence of clear rivalries between these two groups, it was incorrect to speak of them as two distinct entities.

Which view is supported by the data? On the one hand, all of the corporations believed to have been controlled by both groups fit into the same clique. Standard Oil, National City Bank, Kuhn, Loeb, and Union Pacific, as well as the corporations they controlled, were all members of the huge Morgan clique. Furthermore, George W. Perkins, a J. P. Morgan partner, a vice-president of the Morgan-controlled New York Life, and a director in several Morgan-controlled corporations, sat on the board of Stillman's National City Bank. And Charles Steele, a Morgan partner, sat on the board of the Baltimore & Ohio, a firm believed to have been under Kuhn, Loeb influence (Daggett, 1908).

Nevertheless, except for these two cases, nearly all corporations directly linked with J. P. Morgan & Co. were believed to be under Morgan control. These included industrials such as U.S. Steel (3 Morgan directors), International Harvester (2), and General Electric (1); railroads such as the Reading (2), Lehigh Valley (2), and Erie (1); and financials such as New York Life, National Bank of Commerce, and First National Bank. Similarly, members of the "Rockefeller-Stillman-Schiff-Harriman alliance" consistently interlocked with one another, as well as with their subordinate companies. Thus, Kuhn, Loeb partners sat on the boards of National City Bank, Union Pacific, Equitable Life, Equitable Trust, and Baltimore & Ohio. Standard Oil sent two officers and received one from Amalgamated Copper, and sent two officers to both National City and Union Pacific. Still, although only National City Bank interlocked directly with J. P. Morgan & Co., there was considerable interlocking among all four firms in the alliance and companies under Morgan control. For example, two Kuhn, Loeb partners sat on the board of National Bank of Commerce; Union Pacific had a representative on the board of the Reading; Standard Oil had two of its officers on the board of U.S. Steel; and National City had officer interlocks with New York Life and International Harvester. Thus, both positions are partially correct.

An interpretation which is consistent with both of these positions is that the two groups, while still distinguishable, had begun to temper, or institutionalize, their conflicts. This can be illustrated by citing the famous 1901 battle for control of the Northern Pacific Railroad between J. J. Hill (backed by Morgan) and Harriman (backed by Schiff of Kuhn, Loeb). When Harriman attempted to purchase the stock of the railroad, a move strongly opposed by Morgan, a battle ensued which pushed the price up to record levels, nearly precipitating a major economic catastrophe (Allen, 1935; Sobel, 1965; Carosso, 1970). Eventually, a compromise was reached in which control was to be shared by Morgan and Harriman, while Hill would continue to operate the railroad. Thus by 1904 we see the two interests both strongly represented on the Great Northern-Northern Pacific board. Harriman, Schiff, and Stillman all had seats, as did Morgan allies Perkins and George F. Baker (First National Bank). This case set a precedent which was later to be widely followed: the sharing of corporate control by a plurality of external influences. The idea of limiting "destructive competition" was a clear goal of Morgan's. To restate the words of Cochran and Miller (1961: 196-197) in discussing Morgan's plans for reorganizing and combining railroads: "A general 'community of interest' must be established among major companies so that costly competition would be replaced by cooperation." The "community of interest" idea took on such significance that by 1907 Morgan had become one of the major stockholders in the National City Bank (Sobel, 1965; Carosso, 1970).

To return to the peak analysis for subsequent years, both 1912 and 1919 show almost identical results. In 1912 there is a single huge clique of 125 corporations, with First National Bank as its peak (J. P. Morgan & Co. is a close second in centrality). There are also 2 small cliques of 3 and 2 members, respectively. By 1919, there was 1 clique of 134 corporations led by J. P.

Morgan, and this clique included all interlocked corporations in the strong tie network. The 1912 cluster was very similar to that of 1904. J. P. Morgan & Co. remained strongly tied to First National Bank (5 interlocks), National Bank of Commerce (2), Erie (2), Reading (2), and Great Northern-Northern Pacific (3), and had close ties with 2 banks, Bankers Trust and Guaranty Trust, which were not included in the 1904 sample. These banks were believed to have come under full Morgan control by 1909 (Corey, 1930: 360). In addition, Kuhn, Loeb & Co. maintained its ties to Union Pacific (2 interlocks) and National City Bank (1). J. P. Morgan & Co. also continued its tie to National City Bank. The only changes of any consequence in the network came as a result of the court-ordered dissolution of the Standard Oil trust in 1911, and the severing of most insurance company interlocks after the Armstrong Investigation of 1905. Standard Oil of New Jersey, the main branch of the original trust, had only 3 interlocks in 1912, compared with 25 in 1904. No other descendant of the original Standard Oil had even a single interlock in 1912.

As we saw earlier, by 1919 the network was far less dense than in 1912. However, even the considerable decline in interlocking did not divide the network into distinct cliques. In fact, even the 2 minor cliques from 1912 were absent in 1919. Some of the changes were major. For example, the National Bank of Commerce, the most interlocked corporation in 1904 and 1912 (with 153 and 111, respectively), had only 10 interlocks by 1919. The Commerce Bank had previously established itself as a meeting place for the directors of major New York financial institutions. For example, in 1904, officers of 13 major New York financial corporations, including 6 banks, sat on the Commerce Bank board. In 1912, officers of 10 major New York financials sat on the Commerce board. By 1919, New York banks could no longer interlock with one another, and the Commerce Bank's centrality declined considerably. At the same time, ties between many major banks and investment houses were severed, even though they had not been outlawed.

Still, a look at J. P. Morgan & Co.'s interlocks reveals that the firm maintained its ties to most of the same corporations. Aside from strong links to Bankers Trust and Guaranty Trust, Morgan maintained its ties with Great Northern-Northern Pacific, Pullman, U.S. Steel, International Harvester, General Electric, and Reading.[2] Morgan also established ties to the rapidly growing copper mining companies, Kennecott and Utah Copper, and a link to General Motors, which was just then getting on its feet.[3]

At the same time, the distinctions between the two major groups of the 1904-1912 period became even more blurred. While Morgan was not tied to Anaconda Copper, the successor to the Rockefeller-controlled Amalgamated Copper, and although Anaconda shared a director with National City Bank, it also placed one of its officers on the board of Morgan ally Guaranty Trust. In addition, Standard Oil of New Jersey placed one of its two interlocking directors on the board of Guaranty Trust (the other was with Equitable Trust). The Kuhn, Loeb tie with Union Pacific remained, and the Chase National Bank, led at the time by Morgan ally Albert H. Wiggin, remained linked (as it had in 1912) with such Morgan-dominated firms as New York Life, Seaboard Air Line, and International Harvester.

In sum, while the 1912-1919 period saw a number of changes in the density of interlocking and in the evolution of institutional rather than individual control of corporations (see Chapter 7), the network as a whole continued to lack any kind of clique structure. In most cases, the alliances that existed in 1904 remained in 1919.

The Emergence of Cliques: 1935-1974

In 1935, for the first time, a clique structure emerged. Both the nonweighted and weighted (directional) networks yielded cliques in the 4 years. However, in certain cases one measure produced one very large group while the other yielded several smaller ones. For example, in 1964 the strong tie network produced 8 cliques, ranging in size from 2 to 12 members. But although the directional network produced 6 cliques, the largest contained 67 members, and 4 of the remaining 5 had but 2 members each. The strong tie Mellon Bank clique had 8 members, while the directional had 67. This is indicative of the type of problem encountered as a result of the extreme sensitivity of the criteria for peak analysis (see Chapter 3). It was dealt with here by a decision to employ the results most characteristic with what we would expect based on the theoretical concept of interest groups. Thus, the strong tie network cliques were analyzed in 1935, 1964, and 1969, while the directional cliques were employed in 1974. Cliques produced by the alternative criteria for each year are presented in the Appendix.

The 1935 strong tie network includes 37 isolates. Among the 130 interlocked corporations are 6 peaks, 3 of which are contained within the large, 122-member component. The remaining peaks are at the heads of components of 3, 3, and 2 members, respectively. I shall refer to cliques within the large component as "major" cliques, and those in individual small components as "minor" cliques. In all, only 22 corporations were actual clique members (only 14 within the major component), while 108 corporations were "mixed" members, including 6 bridges. The members of the 6 cliques are listed in Table 6.3. Groups 1-3 are major cliques, while 4-6 are minor cliques. The individual members are listed in order of descending centrality.

In a number of cases, historical evidence suggests that the members of the particular cliques are accurately situated. For example, in the Morgan group, Bankers Trust was organized and controlled by J. P. Morgan (Corey, 1930) and is believed to have remained a Morgan ally at least through the late 1960s (Kotz, 1978). Kennecott Copper was under strong Morgan influence through stock ownership (Corey, 1930; TNEC, 1940) and used Morgan as its principal bank (Pecora, 1939: 14). Baldwin Locomotive, in receivership during the Depression, was also believed to be a Morgan-controlled firm (Corey, 1930).

On the other hand, there were other firms for which the evidence of Morgan influence was less clear. For example, the Boston & Maine had been controlled by Morgan early in the century through the New York, New Haven, and Hartford.

Table 6.3 Peak Analysis Cliques, 1935

(1) J. P. Morgan & Co.
       (New York)
     Bankers Trust (New York)
     Kennecott Copper (New York)
     Philadelphia & Reading Coal &
       Iron (Philadelphia)
     Baldwin Locomotive
       (Philadelphia)
     International Paper (Boston)
     White, Weld & Co. (New York)
     Boston & Maine (Boston)

(2) Mutual Life Ins. (New York)
     First National Bank
       (New York)
     Southern Railway (Richmond)
     Lehigh Coal & Navigation
       (Philadelphia)

(3) Crown Zellerbach
       (San Francisco)
     Blyth & Co. (San Francisco)

(4) Climax Molybdenum
       (New York)
     American Metal (New York)
     C. M. Loeb & Co. (New York)

(5) American I.G. Chemical
       (New York)
     Ford Motor (Detroit)
     Standard Oil of NJ (New York)

(6) Wheeling Steel (Wheeling)
     Seaboard Air Line (Richmond)

However, in 1913 a scandal developed when it was revealed that, under J. P. Morgan's direction, the New Haven board had been buying up a number of competitors at extremely high prices while cutting back dividend payments significantly. By the time J. P. Morgan & Co. withdrew as fiscal agents for the New Haven, dividends had been suspended entirely and Morgan himself was indicted for conspiracy (Corey, 1930). By 1935 the New Haven had become part of the Pennsylvania system, which had strong ties to Kuhn, Loeb & Co. Philadelphia and Reading

Coal & Iron was also not under direct Morgan influence; 21.7 percent of P&R's stock was owned by the Baltimore & Ohio, and the stock was pledged to National City Bank. And International Paper was believed to be controlled by the Phipps family of Boston and the Chase National Bank (Sweezy, 1953). White, Weld & Co. was an investment bank which around the turn of the century had performed certain services for J. P. Morgan & Co. (Redlich, 1951: 376); however, there is no evidence of a continuing relationship into the 1930s.

The Mutual Life group, containing the First National Bank, should, according to some accounts, be considered part of the Morgan group (Sweezy, 1953; Allen, 1978). Both firms were considered Morgan allies. Southern Railway was a family-controlled firm (the Millbanks) with ownership ties to the Harrimans and J. P. Morgan & Co., and Lehigh Coal & Navigation had ownership ties to both Chase National Bank and Guaranty Trust (TNEC, 1940). In fact, the two groups overlap considerably. A total of 108 corporations were mixed members between the 2 cliques. Among these were 6 bridges: U.S. Steel, Guaranty Trust, General Motors, Northern Pacific, Reading, and Penn Mutual Life. Of these 6, only Penn Mutual was not considered to be under Morgan influence. U.S. Steel remained under Morgan influence at least into the 1930s (Josephson, 1972). Guaranty Trust was a Morgan ally; Northern Pacific was under Morgan influence dating back to the 1890s; and General Motors, although dominated by the Du Ponts, was also strongly influenced by J. P. Morgan & Co. The Reading had been reorganized by J. P. Morgan in the 1890s; however, there is no evidence to indicate Morgan influence in the 1930s. Overall, 4 of these 6 bridges were included in the Morgan cliques identified by both Sweezy and Allen.

But only 2 of the 4 remaining 1935 cliques contain meaningful groupings, and both of these were minor cliques, and hence were isolated from the rest of the network. Clique 4 contains 3 closely linked firms; 12 percent of Climax Molybdenum stock was owned by the Loeb family, and 8.9 percent by American Metal. And 2.6 percent of American Metal stock was owned by

C. M. Loeb & Co. (TNEC, 1940). According to the ·TNEC report (1940: 109), these three corporations were controlled by the Hochschild, Sussman, and Loeb families. Clique 5 contains Standard Oil of New Jersey, generally believed to have been under Rockefeller family control. Standard Oil was a major stockholder in American I.G. Chemical (TNEC, 1940: 143). However, Ford Motor was 100 percent owned and controlled by Henry Ford and family, and there is no evidence of an alliance with the Rockefellers. Furthermore, the other members of the Rockefeller oil empire were absent from this group, and, like Standard Oil (NJ), were not heavily interlocked. Among the major oil companies dominated by the Rockefellers (all through large stockholdings), only Jersey and Socony Vacuum Oil Company (forerunner of Mobil) were interlocked within the system, with 1 and 2 ties, respectively. The other 4, Standard of Indiana, Standard of California, Atlantic, and Ohio Oil, were all isolates. Furthermore, while Chase National Bank, considered part of the Rockefeller sphere of influence, interlocked with such firms as Socony Vacuum, Equitable Life, Metropolitan Life, and International Paper (all considered at least partly Rockefeller controlled), it did not interlock with any of the remaining Standard Oil companies. Yet Chase did interlock with such supposedly Morgan-dominated firms as Kennecott and the Northern Pacific, and was a mixed member between the Morgan and Mutual cliques.

Thus, when the Morgan and Mutual-First National Bank groups are combined, the picture in 1935 is not much different from that in the 1904-1919 period. The network is not as dense as in earlier periods (in 1935 it was only about one-half as dense as in 1912) and this relative sparseness increases the likelihood of separate groups appearing. But the groups which do appear are not distinct enough to represent major cleavages within the system. In 1935, despite the increased visibility of Rockefeller-influenced corporations, the system was still very much dominated by J. P. Morgan & Co.

However, by 1964 things had changed. First, different parts of the country (such as Pittsburgh, Chicago, and California) became more widely represented, as the complete domination of New York began to recede. Second, a large number of new industrial corporations attained prominence in the network. And third, the First National City Bank (Citibank) emerged as a major independent bank. The cliques generated for the years 1964, 1969, and 1974 are presented in Table 6.4.

By 1964, there was a total of 8 separate cliques in the network, 4 of which (5-8) are separate components (minor groups); 3 of these are pairs of 2 firms each. The remaining 4 cliques fall within a large component of 135 corporations, only 29 of which are actual clique members. However, this is far more than the 14 members in 1935. Among the significant developments by 1964 are 2 major cliques (and 3 minor ones) with their centers outside New York, compared with none (and 2 minors) in 1935. These include a large Mellon Bank (Pittsburgh) group and a First National Bank (Chicago) group. Furthermore, even the New York-dominated Citibank group contains 4 non-New York firms among its 12 members. Also, the composition of the groups changed considerably between 1935 and 1964. The Morgan and Mutual Life cliques, the 2 major groups in 1935, no longer constitute specific entities. Rather, the two largest 1964 groups are based around Citibank and Mellon National Bank. Kennecott, a member of the Morgan group in 1935, is a member of the Citibank group in 1964, and International Paper is a member of the Chase group in 1964.

How plausible are the 1964 cliques? It should be pointed out that, compared to the earlier years, by the 1960s this question is much more difficult to answer. Nevertheless, one group of undeniable significance is the Mellon group. The five Pittsburgh-based industrials, Gulf, Jones & Laughlin Steel, Aluminum Co. of America (Alcoa), Westinghouse, and Pittsburgh Plate Glass, have long ties to the Mellon family and the Mellon Bank. For example, in 1964, Mellon National Bank owned 25.3 percent of Alcoa stock and 17.1 percent of Gulf Oil stock. The Mellon Bank also managed pension funds for PPG and Westinghouse (Allen, 1978). Mellon was also a major stockholder in Jones & Laughlin Steel before unloading its stock in 1967 after

Table 6.4 Peak Analysis Cliques, 1964-1974

1964

(1) Mellon National Bank
        (Pittsburgh)
      Gulf Oil (Pittsburgh)
      Jones & Laughlin Steel
        (Pittsburgh)
      Westinghouse Electric
        (Pittsburgh)
      Aluminum Co. of America
        (Pittsburgh)
      United California Bank
        (Los Angeles)
      Lockheed Aircraft
        (Los Angeles)

(2) Chase Manhattan Bank
        (New York)
      American Airlines (New York)
      Martin-Marietta (New York)
      International Paper
        (New York)

(3) First National City Bank
        (New York)
      United Aircraft (Hartford)
      Kimberly-Clark (Milwaukee)
      Allied Chemical (New York)
      Standard Oil of NJ (New York)
      International Tel. & Tel.
        (New York)
      W. R. Grace (New York)
      Northwestern Mutual Life
        (Milwaukee)
      Chicago, Milwaukee & St. Paul
        (Chicago)
      Kennecott Copper (New York)
      Sinclair Oil (New York)
      Merrill, Lynch (New York)

(4) First National Bank (Chicago)
      Caterpillar Tractor (Peoria)
      Chicago & Northwestern
        (Chicago)
      Armour & Co. (Chicago)
      Shell Oil (New York)

Table 6.4 Continued

1964

(5) New York Central (Albany)
    Smith, Barney & Co.
      (New York)

(6) National Bank of Detroit
      (Detroit)
    Dow Chemical (Detroit)
    National Steel ((Pittsburgh)

(7) Firestone Tire & Rubber
      (Akron)
    Cleveland Trust (Cleveland)

(8) Burlington Industries
      (Greensboro)
    R. J. Reynolds Tobacco
      (Winston-Salem)

1969

(1) First National City Bank
      (New York)
    Metropolitan Life (New York)
    Monsanto (St. Louis)
    W. R. Grace (New York)
    Boeing Aircraft (Seattle)
    International Tel. & Tel.
      (New York)
    Du Pont (Wilmington)
    Crocker National Bank
      (San Francisco)
    Standard Oil of California
      (Los Angeles)

(2) Morgan Guaranty Trust
      (New York)
    Aetna Life (Hartford)
    Procter & Gamble (Cincinnati)
    Control Data Corp.
      (Minneapolis)
    Santa Fe Industries (Chicago)

(3) Chemical Bank (New York)
    Borden (New York)
    McDonnell-Douglas (St. Louis)
    Western Electric (New York)
    Seaboard Coast Line
      (Richmond)

(Continued)

Table 6.4 Continued

1969

(4) Chase Manhattan Bank
       (New York)
     Burlington Industries
       (Greensboro)
     R. J. Reynolds Tobacco
       (Winston-Salem)

(5) Mellon National Bank
       (Pittsburgh)
     Gulf Oil (Pittsburgh)
     PPG Industries (Pittsburgh)
     North American Rockwell
       (Los Angeles)

1974

(1) J. P. Morgan & Co.
       (New York)
     Aetna Life (Hartford)
     Exxon (New York)
     Coca-Cola Co. (Atlanta)
     Western Electric (New York)
     Procter & Gamble (Cincinnati)
     United Aircraft (Hartford)
     Southern Railway (Richmond)
     Prudential Insurance (Boston)
     TRW (Cleveland)
     Travelers Insurance (Hartford)
     Eastman Kodak (Rochester)
     Delta Airlines (Atlanta)

(2) Celanese (New York)
     Bankers Trust (New York)
     Anaconda Copper (New York)
     Metropolitan Life (New York)
     Mobil Oil (New York)
     Union Pacific (New York)
     R. J. Reynolds
       (Winston-Salem)
     Crocker National Bank
       (San Francisco)
     American Can (New York)
     Continental Airlines
       (Los Angeles)

Table 6.4 Continued

	1974
(3)	Manufacturers Hanover Trust (New York)
	Kraftco (New York)
	B. F. Goodrich (New York)
	Goldman, Sachs & Co. (New York)
	Chrysler (Detroit)
	LTV (Dallas)
(4)	Honeywell (Minneapolis)
	Northwest Airlines (Minneapolis)
(5)	National Bank of Detroit (Detroit)
	American Airlines (New York)
(6)	Dow Chemical (Detroit)
	Missouri Pacific (St. Louis)
(7)	Atlantic-Richfield (New York) (peak with no clique members)

James Ling of LTV took over Jones & Laughlin. Furthermore, Mellon's ties to Lockheed Aircraft may have been a reflection of its strong interest in the aerospace industry (Menshikov, 1969: 302).

The Chase Manhattan group (group 2 in Table 6.4) also includes corporations generally believed to be either controlled or influenced by Chase. A House subcommittee investigation in the early 1960s revealed that American Airlines was under strong Rockefeller influence (Menshikov, 1969: 270-271). International Paper has long ties to Chase (Sweezy, 1953; Menshikov, 1969). And Martin-Marietta is considered to be influenced by both Chase and Mellon (Menshikov, 1969).

However, the evidence of control or influence in recent years is far more controversial and less clear than that for the earlier years. For example, the Citibank group includes several firms considered under Citibank control, but others for which con-

trary or no evidence exists. Of the nine nonfinancial corporations in the Citibank clique, six are thought by Menshikov
(1969) to be members of that group. These include United
Aircraft, Kimberly-Clark, Allied Chemical, ITT, W. R. Grace,
and Kennecott. However, of these six, only one (Kimberly-
Clark) was not classified simultaneously within another major
financial group by Menshikov.

A more systematic and reliable analysis of the 1964-1974
cliques can be made by referring to the study by Kotz (1978) as
well as the Menshikov study. Both studies attempt to classify
members of different interest groups, and both rely almost
exclusively on evidence other than interlocks. The two studies
have very different approaches. Kotz is concerned with what he
sees as direct control of nonfinancial corporations by particular
financial corporations. His criteria are based mostly on stockholdings by bank trust departments in particular firms (see
Chapter 2 for a complete description of Kotz's criteria for
control). Some of his evidence also comes from loan data. In
general, Kotz's classificatory scheme is extremely stringent. In
the face of any doubt about the locus of control, he classified
the firm as "not under an identifiable source of control."

Menshikov, on the other hand, takes a more general and less
precise approach. Any nonfinancials in which certain financials
appear to have an interest or some type of stable business
relationship are grouped together. Thus, many firms are members of two or more groups.

In this section, we will observe the extent to which the
findings of the peak analysis correspond to those of Menshikov
and Kotz. Menshikov's data cover several different years in the
1960s, while Kotz's focus is on the period from 1967 through
1969. Since the period under investigation here is 1964-1974,
there may have been transfers of affiliation and/or control
during these periods. Any such cases will be mentioned whenever applicable. Table 6.5 presents an examination of the relation between Menshikov's and Kotz's findings and those of the
peak analysis from the present study.

TABLE 6.5 Comparison of Peak Analysis Clique Members with
Classifications of Kotz and Menshikov

	1964		1969		1974	
Peak Analysis	*K*	*M*	*K*	*M*	*K*	*M*
Same Classification	7	11	4	12	2	12
Different Classification	13	3	14	6	14	3

As the table indicates, the peak analysis classifications are
very similar to those of Menshikov, and very different from
those of Kotz. This suggests that during the 1964-1974 period,
the cliques are indicative of strong intercorporate ties, but not
clearly of control relations. This is consistent with the finding
on banks in Chapter 5, in which their continuing significance
appeared to stem more from their centrality in the network
than from direct control relations with nonfinancials.

Comparison of Peak Analysis with Factor Analysis

Considering the ambiguity of the results of the peak analysis
when compared with external criteria, this section will consist
of a direct comparison of the results produced by Allen's
(1978) factor analysis of 1970 data and the peak analysis for
1969. The basis for the comparison is not a perfect one. Allen's
data consist of the largest 200 nonfinancial corporations and
the 50 largest financial corporations, based on asset rank. My
data consist of 125 nonfinancials and 42 financials. My data,
unlike Allen's, include investment banks, while Allen's include
utilities and retailers. Nevertheless, for the present purposes, the
data sets are roughly comparable.[4]

In order to determine the connections among corporations
within Allen's cliques, I utilized the 1969 data set collected by
Mariolis (1975). This set includes 797 corporations, including
all 250 of Allen's firms. In a few cases there were discrepancies
between the 2 data sets, as, for example, when I found that a

TABLE 6.6 Characteristics of Factor Analysis Cliques

Clique (type)	Size	Density	Centrifugality
(1) Chemical Bank (G)	6	.800	.258
(2) Continental Illinois (G)	9	.528	.477
(3) Mellon National Bank (fam.)	5	.800	.519
(4) Morgan Guaranty (F)	7	.524	.226
(5) First National City (F)	7	.571	.204
(6) Republic Steel (G or F)	8	.821	.331
(7) Chase Manhattan (G)	5	1.000	.194
(8) Western Bancorp. (G)	7	.667	.400
(9) Pennsylvania Mutual (G)	6	.600	.583
(10) National Bank of Det. (G)	6	.600	.508
Average (weighted)	6.6	.661	.336

NOTE: G = geographical; F = financial; fam. = family.

company had 10 interlocks with other group members but Allen credited the firm with only 9. In these cases I assumed that there were more interlocks in the Mariolis sample because of additional links through third parties not included in the smaller Allen sample. In all such cases I employed Allen's calculation.

The 10 cliques identified by Allen averaged 6.6 members each. In nearly all of the groups, most of the corporations were located in the same geographical area. Only one group (Mellon) was classified as a family-based interest group, and just 2 others (Morgan Guaranty Trust and Citibank) were classified as financially based groups. A group which includes Chemical Bank was considered possibly a financial group. The remaining 6 groups were viewed as purely geographical, although Allen noted that many of the groups included financial connections between the banks and nonfinancials. The peak analysis and factor analysis groups will be compared on the basis of size, density, and "centrifugality," as well as correspondence with independent evidence.[5] Table 6.6 presents the first 3 of the above characteristics for the 10 groups identified by Allen. The groups are identified by the corporation with the highest principal component score within the group.

The first point of interest is the fact that in all but one of the groups a financial corporation produced the highest loading, despite the fact that only two of the groups were considered financially based. However, when the high density of the groups is observed, the case for viewing them in a nonhierarchical fashion becomes more plausible. The average weighted density of the six geographical groups (based on the total number of within-group links divided by the possible number of within-group links summed across cliques) is .652, while the density for the 2 financial groups is .548. According to the discussion in Chapter 4, we should expect the geographical groups to have higher density than the financial groups. And in Allen's results this is indeed the case, although the differences are not large. An example of one of Allen's geographical cliques is presented in Figure 6.1.

In this example, the position of highest centrality is shared by Chemical Bank and Consolidated Edison, both of which are tied to all 5 remaining firms (although Chemical has a total of 12 interlocks with the other 5 companies, compared to Con Ed's 11). Meanwhile, 2 other corporations, New York Life and Southern Pacific, are linked with 4 of the 5 other points in the clique. Borden and Equitable, the 2 least central members of the group, have links to 3 other group members. This is a good example of a clique based on structural equivalence groupings. No one corporation is dominant, and the clique is highly dense (.800). As Allen's evidence suggests, there is no indication that this clique in any way constitutes a financial interest group led by Chemical. If anything, the group appears to be a configuration of coequals.

However, even the cliques designated by Allen as financial groups do not produce structures commensurate with unqualified bank dominance. Figure 6.2 presents a graph of the Citibank clique. In this group, only Citibank is tied to every other corporation. However, the only reason for this is its link to the

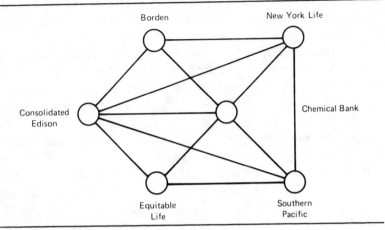

Figure 6.1 **Chemical Bank Clique (Factor Analysis)**

otherwise isolated American Telephone & Telegraph. Except for this one difference, Monsanto (with five links) is as central within the group as Citibank. In addition, Pan American is linked to four other corporations, and Kimberly-Clark and NCR to three each. Thus, even a supposedly financially based clique such as the Citibank group does not have the kind of structure normally associated with the domination of a particular corporation.

Judging from the character of Allen's cliques, it appears that the assumption of structural equivalence leads to a set of relatively balanced, highly dense, and nonhierarchical clique formations. This type of clique is substantively similar to the concept of geographically based interest groups, in which no one corporation clearly dominates.

Peak Analysis Results

For the peak analysis I will use the strong tie network as mentioned earlier. The strong tie network produced 5 cliques, each led by a bank. The cliques averaged 5.2 members com-

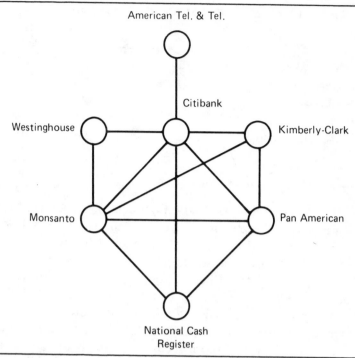

American Tel. & Tel.

Citibank

Westinghouse

Kimberly-Clark

Monsanto

Pan American

National Cash
Register

Figure 6.2 First National City Bank Clique (Factor Analysis)

pared to Allen's 6.6, yet their density was considerably lower (.400 compared to Allen's .661). This is significant because the density of a clique is partly a function of its size. The number of possible connections increases geometrically with each additional member. Table 6.7 presents the characteristics of the peak analysis cliques.[6]

To compare the peak analysis cliques with those of factor analysis, I have provided some examples of the clique structure from the peak analysis. Figure 6.3 is a graphic representation of the Chemical Bank group. It should be compared with Figure 6.1. Notice that the structure of Figure 6.3 is almost identical to the "X" formation, the structure of maximum possible hierarchy. The Citibank clique, pictured in Figure 6.4, follows a

TABLE 6.7 Characteristics of Peak Analysis Cliques (Strong Tie)

Clique (type)	Size	Density	Cent.
(1) Morgan Guaranty	5	.400	.125
(2) First National City	9	.278	.184
(3) Chemical Bank	5	.500	.194
(4) Chase Manhattan	3	1.000	.158
(5) Mellon National Bank	4	.667	.415
Average (weighted)	5.2	.400	.200

similar pattern (compare with Figure 6.2). Again the clique resembles an X, with Citibank clearly the most central point. While Citibank is tied to six of the other eight members of the clique, only Boeing (with three ties) is linked to more than two. The densities of the Chemical and Citibank factor analysis cliques are .800 and .571, respectively, compared with .500 and .278 for the peak analysis cliques, but the latter groups were closer to the structure predicted by a financial control model. The question is, which more accurately depicts the actual relations among the corporations? To help answer this question, I shall compare the data with the studies by Menshikov and Kotz.

Of the 2 cliques classified as financial groups by Allen (Morgan Guaranty and Citibank), 11 of the 12 nonfinancial corporations were assigned to those groups by Menshikov (Table 6.8). Of the criteria used to determine group membership, only 2 of the 11 were based primarily on directorship ties. However, it should be noted that Menshikov classifies a number of corporations as members of 2 or more groups. Of these 11 corporations, 8 were in fact placed in 2 or more groups by Menshikov. Furthermore, in the Kotz study, only 2 of the 11 corporations were classified as controlled by the banks in their respective interlock groups. Both of these firms, General Electric and Scott Paper, were members of the Morgan group. Not a single member of Allen's Citibank clique was considered by Kotz to be Citibank-controlled.

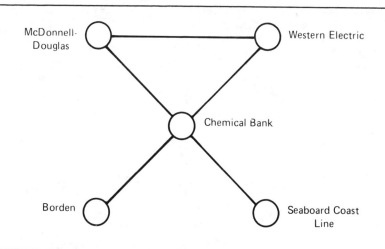

Figure 6.3 Chemical Bank Clique (Peak Analysis)

In the peak analysis, of the nine corporations in the Morgan and Citibank groups, six were assigned to those groups by Menshikov, while only two of the nine were placed there by Kotz. Thus, both measures fare approximately the same when compared with the classifications of Menshikov and Kotz, very well according to Menshikov's scheme, but rather poorly when compared with Kotz's. The relatively poor showing on Kotz's criteria may be the result of a difference in focus. As mentioned above, Kotz was attempting to determine which corporations were *controlled* by specific banks (control meaning the ability to determine the long-run policies of a corporation), and his criteria were extremely stringent. When in doubt, Kotz classified corporations as "not under an identifiable source of control." Menshikov's classifications, on the other hand, were based on close relations between corporations and banks, which may or may not have been control relations. Since a number of large corporations do business with several banks, Menshikov was far more likely to find corporations closely linked with two or more banks. This perspective is closer to the concept of relative influence in the network advanced in Chapter 2.

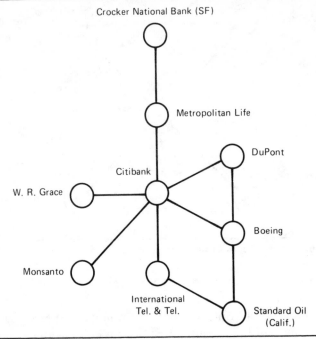

Figure 6.4 First National City Bank Clique (Peak Analysis)

Nevertheless, the wide disparities between Menshikov's and Kotz's classifications are disturbing. Under normal circumstances, the fact that Menshikov's results are similar to those of the interlock studies would increase the validity of all three. However, as shown in Table 6.9, there is very little correspondence between the factor analysis and the peak analysis results. Of the eighteen nonfinancial members of the five peak analysis cliques, only five are members of the corresponding factor analysis groups. Only the Mellon group is very similar on the two measures. Similar problems exist in other years as well. For example, Anaconda Copper, which, prior to its takeover by Arco in 1977, was believed to have been controlled by Chase Manhattan, is a member of the Celanese group in 1974. This might appear plausible, since Kotz sees Celanese as controlled by Chase. But the bank in the Celanese group is not Chase, but Bankers Trust, a supposed Morgan ally.

TABLE 6.8 Classification of Nonfinancial Corporations According to
Menshikov and Kotz (Morgan, Citibank Cliques)

A. Factor Analysis Cliques	classifications	
Morgan Group	*Menshikov*	*Kotz*
General Motors	Morgan[a,b]	none
General Electric	Morgan[a]	Morgan[a,b]
Continental Oil	Morgan	none
Scott Paper	Morgan[a]	Morgan[a]
U.S. Steel	Morgan[a,b]	none
Procter & Gamble	Morgan[a]	none
Citibank Group		
Monsanto	Citibank	Chase
NCR	Citibank[a]	Morgan[a]
Westinghouse	Citibank[a]	Mellon[a,c]
Kimberly-Clark	Citibank	Schweitzer family
Pan-American	Citibank[a]	none
American Tel. & Tel.	Chase[a]	none

B. Peak Analysis Cliques (Strong Tie)	classifications	
Morgan Group	*Menshikov*	*Kotz*
Procter & Gamble	Morgan[a]	none
Control Data Corp.	no info.	Morgan (thru Bankers Trust)
Santa Fe Industries	no info.	none
Citibank Group		
Monsanto	Citibank	Chase
W. R. Grace	Citibank[a]	Citibank[a]
Boeing	Citibank	Chase
International Tel. & Tel.	Citibank[a]	Lazard Freres[a]
DuPont	DuPonts	DuPonts
Standard Oil (California)	Citibank[a]	none

SOURCES: Menshikov (1969); Kotz (1978); for factor analysis groups, Allen (1978).

a. Also placed in other groups.

b. Classification based primarily on interlock evidence.

c. Westinghouse was also a member of Allen's Mellon clique.

One reason for this kind of finding is the low centrifugality in
the cliques on both measures (Tables 6.6 and 6.7). In nearly all
cases, the great majority of interlocks occur with corporations
outside the cliques, but this finding is interpreted in different

Table 6.9 Comparison of Peak Analysis Cliques with Corresponding Factor
Analysis Cliques

_____

Peak Analysis
_____

(1) Morgan Guaranty Trust
     Aetna Life Insurance
     Procter & Gamble
     Control Data Corp.
     Santa Fe Industries

(2) First National City Bank
     Metropolitan Life Insurance
     Monsanto
     W. R. Grace
     Boeing Aircraft
     International Tel. & Tel.
     DuPont
     Standard Oil (California)
     Crocker National Bank
         (San Francisco)

(3) Chemical Bank
     Borden
     McDonell-Douglas
     Western Electric
     Seaboard Coast Line

(4) Chase Manhattan Bank
     Burlington Industries
     R. J. Reynolds Tobacco

(5) Mellon National Bank
     Gulf Oil
     PPG Industries
     North American Aviation

Factor Analysis
_____

(1) Morgan Guaranty Trust
     General Electric
     General Motors
     Continental Oil
     Scott Paper
     U.S. Steel
     Proctor & Gamble
_____

Table 6.9 Continued

Factor Analysis

(2) First National City Bank
Monsanto
National Cash Register
Westinghouse
Kimberly-Clark
Pan American World Airways
American Tel. & Tel.

(3) Chemical Bank
New York Life Insurance
Consolidated Edison
Southern Pacific
Equitable Life Assurance
Borden

(4) Chase Manhattan Bank
General Foods
Metropolitan Life Insurance
International Paper
American Tel. & Tel.

(5) Mellon National Bank
Gulf Oil
PPG Industries
Aluminum Co. of America
Westinghouse

SOURCE: For factor analysis, Allen (1978: 608-609).

ways by the two approaches. In factor analysis, the points outside the cliques are virtually ignored. As White et al. (1976: 736) note in discussing traditional sociometric methods: "Persons not in cliques are usually disregarded (i.e., treated as outside the effective sociometric system)." In the peak analysis, on the other hand, most of the corporations (119 of the 145 nonisolates) are classified as mixed members, within the sphere of certain groups but not clearly members of any one. This

presents a very different view of the system from that presented
by the factor analysis. The peak analysis suggests a tightly
connected system with a few points of particular significance
(the 5 peaks) and a few specific clusters, but with most corporations falling somewhere between or among the different peaks.
Of the 119 contested members, only 27 were within the sphere
of 2 groups, while 46 were mixed among 3, 28 among 4, and 18
corporations were within the purview of all 5 cliques. This
finding is very close to that reported by Menshikov, who classified the majority of his corporations within 2 or more groups. It
also provides us with a picture of a network so tightly connected that the cliques do not form a major part of it. Its
overriding characteristic is the overlapping *among* the various
cliques, again a conclusion not perceivable from the factor
analysis results. This gives peak analysis an advantage in understanding the role of cliques within the larger network.

Discussion

Rather than a system of several distinct cliques which
disintegrates over time, the evidence presented here reveals one
large cluster from 1904 to 1919, which begins to separate into
cliques in 1935 and remains "cliquified" through 1974. There
appear to be two principal explanations for this trend. First, the
appearance of cliques in the network corresponds with the
decline in the dominance of J. P. Morgan & Co. In the early
1900s, as we have seen, J. P. Morgan was clearly the most
important figure in the economy. After his death, in 1913, his
firm maintained its unquestioned dominance at least into the
1920s. However, by the 1930s other groups had begun to equal
the Morgan firm in power.

Prior to the 1920s, Morgan's chief rivals were Rockefeller and
Harriman. Harriman died in 1908, and although his descendants
remained in control of the Union Pacific and later gained
control of Brown Brothers & Co., a private commercial bank,
they never approached the influence of the original Harriman.
The Rockefellers, meanwhile, although extremely wealthy, did

not prior to 1930 have an overall influence equal to that of Morgan. A reason for this may have been the absence of a major Rockefeller financial institution. Thus, although they were able to independently finance the activities of their industrial corporations (Standard Oil, Amalgamated Copper, Colorado Fuel & Iron, and so on), their powers did not extend beyond their directly controlled companies. Furthermore, although the Rockefellers did forge alliances with Stillman's National City Bank, the latter had by 1907 reached an agreement with Morgan which conceded overall leadership to the latter. It was not until 1930, when the Rockefellers gained control of the Chase National Bank through a merger with Equitable Trust, that Rockefeller influence began to rival that of the Morgan group (Pecora, 1939).

According to Menshikov (1969: 232-233), the decline of Morgan domination can be traced to three main factors. The first, as mentioned above, is the rise of the Rockefellers as a financial group. The second factor is that, as a result of World War I, the United States went from a net debtor to a net creditor. This lessened dependence of a number of American corporations on foreign capital, to which the Morgan bank was uniquely tied. In this sense, the decline of unilateral Morgan dominance can be seen as a consequence of a general strengthening of the American economy in relation to the rest of the world. Finally, the stock market crash of 1929 and the ensuing depression had a major impact on the power of most of the major financial interests. Unlike previous crises, such as in 1907 when J. P. Morgan almost singlehandedly straightened out the stock market, by the 1930s there was no individual capable of wielding such power. Instead, it was the federal government which worked to restore the system.

Corresponding with the decline of Morgan dominance was the rise of other major groups, in both New York and elsewhere. The Rockefeller group, now centered in Chase Manhattan Bank, was alluded to above. Also significant, especially in the 1964-1974 period, were the Citibank, Chemical Bank (which some view as tied to Chase), the Pittsburgh-based Mellon National Bank, and the First National Bank of Chicago.

TABLE 6.10   Clique Memberships, 1935-1974 (Strong Tie)

	1935	1964	1969	1974
Interlocked Firms	130	144	145	135
Peaks	6	8	5	4
Members	22	38	26	86
Mixed Members	108	106	119	49
Among 2 Groups	108	27	27	44
Among 3 Groups	0	11	46	5
Among 4 Groups	0	68	28	18
Among 5 Groups	0	0	18	0

Nevertheless, despite the rise of specific cliques, only a small minority of the corporations in the network fall within the purview of one particular group. The great majority of firms are on the borders between or among several different cliques. The preponderance of mixed memberships and shared lines of influence among major banks corresponds with the growing frequency of loan consortia, with several banks playing key roles in corporate financing (Mintz and Schwartz, 1980). Table 6.10 presents a description of the number of peaks, clique members, and mixed memberships from 1935-1974. An interesting phenomenon in the strong tie network is the apparent coalescence in 1974. However, this finding is considerably different in the directional network, suggesting that the alterations were an artifact of the measure.

Furthermore, the cohesiveness and exclusiveness of the cliques was generally low and did not follow a pattern over time. Table 6.11 lists the average size, density, and centrifugality for the 1935-1974 cliques (all strong tie except 1974). The figures fluctuate widely with no clear patterns (they are apparently highly sensitive to the wide variations in the peak analysis results). The low density is, as we have seen, consistent with the assumptions of peak analysis. But in all cases, the great majority of members' interlocks were with those outside their respective cliques, further demonstrating the considerable overlap and blurred boundaries among the cliques.

TABLE 6.11   Characteristics of Peak Analysis Cliques, 1935-1974

	ST 1935	ST 1964	ST 1969	Dir 1974
Density	.452	.373	.400	.291
Centrifugality	.268	.360	.200	.326
Average Size	3.7	4.8	5.2	5.8
Number of Groups	6	8	5	6

NOTE: ST = strong tie network; Dir = directional network.

Geographical Versus Financial

Because of the incomplete nature of our data on financial relationships, the hypothesis of increasing geographical similarity can best be examined by looking at the geographical correspondence of clique members in the four periods. This was done by comparing the number of corporations whose principal business offices were located in the same city or metropolitan area as the peak. Table 6.12 presents a comparison of geographical similarity of clique members for the 1935-1974 period.

As the data indicate, there has been no trend toward increasing geographical similarity of clique members. The only exception to this was 1964, when 75 percent of clique members were in the same geographical areas. This is a consequence of the four relatively well-defined groups in that particular year. As Table 6.4 indicates, six of the eight members of the Mellon Bank group were based in Pittsburgh, all four members of the Chase group and eight of the twelve members of the Citibank group were based in New York, and four of the five First National Chicago members were either Chicago based or, in the case of Caterpillar, based in Peoria. However, as Allen made clear in his study of interest groups, geographical similarity does not necessarily imply that the group lacks a financial basis. This is most obvious in the case of the Mellon group, which is a

TABLE 6.12 Geographical Similarity of Clique Members, 1935-1974

Location	1935	1964	1969	1974
Same Locale as Peak	11	24	12	14
Different Locale	7	8	14	15
Total*	18	32	26	29

* Only cliques of at least three members were included in this calculation.

well-known financial group. Furthermore, as pointed out above, the Chase and Citibank groups also contain a number of financial ties, although in these cases it is not clear that the ties indicate bank control relations.

The final hypothesis suggests that, if the financial nature of interest groups has become less prominent over time, then we should witness a decline in the proportion of peaks which are financials. As Table 6.13 indicates, not only was there not a decline, but through 1969 there was a considerable increase in the proportion of financial peaks. The figure declines in 1974, but remains at a level higher than 1935. The number of peaks is too small for any more than rough statistical comparisons. Nevertheless, it appears that there has been no tendency for cliques to be increasingly centered around nonfinancial corporations.

Conclusion

The phenomenon of specific cliques in the network is a product of the post-1935 era. Prior to that, separate cliques among our 167-firm network did not exist. From 1935-1974, cliques did exist, but even with some alterations of the patterns, the number and size of the groups remained basically stable.

After surveying the cliques and taking into account the large number of corporations not belonging to any particular group, it is difficult to avoid the conclusion that the concept of separate, specific interest groups is not very relevant for understanding the American corporate system. This does not mean

TABLE 6.13   Financial Characteristic of Peaks

	1935 F/T*	1964 F/T	1969 F/T	1974 F/T
Strong Tie Network	2/6	5/8	5/5	3/4
Directional Network	5/9	4/6	6/8	3/7
Total	7/15	9/14	11/13	6/11
% Financials (ST)	33.3	62.5	100.0	75.0
% Financials (Dir)	55.6	66.7	75.0	42.9
% Financials (Total)	46.7	64.3	84.6	54.5

* F/T = financials/total number of peaks

that there are not specific centers of power in the economy, nor does it mean that there are no lasting historical relationships between particular corporations. What it does mean is that the idea that there are several specific groups, regional or otherwise, in which competition forms the basis of their relations, may not be an accurate characterization of the system, if it ever was. Rather, the data indicate that the largest American corporations relate to one another based on a complex system of interdependencies. The sources of this interdependence are several. Nonfinancial corporations are dependent on financials for capital (Zeitlin, 1974). Financials are dependent on other financials because individual banks can no longer provide the financing necessary for most large-scale corporate investments (Mintz and Schwartz, 1980). And members of different industries are dependent on one another for information about general market conditions and potential for their products (Blair, 1976). This, of course, is not meant to suggest that major corporations do not compete, either within or between industries. Nevertheless, given the extent of their common ties, the depth of this competition must be questioned.

NOTES

1. The small size of our sample makes it difficult to thoroughly examine this hypothesis. Herman (1981), for example, argues persuasively that the concentration

of power among the largest firms has increased in recent years. Analyzing only 167 firms does not tell us how these elite companies relate to corporations as a whole. Nevertheless, we know that relations within this group were very unequal early in the century. Their equalization over time would suggest a certain diffusion of power, even if only at the highest levels. Furthermore, managerialists since Berle and Means's time have never denied the high degree of concentration within the business world. Their analyses have almost always been concerned with major corporations. Although a sample larger than the present one would be desirable, the sample here is sufficient for our purposes.

2. A recent article in *Business Week* (March 10, 1980: 40) presented evidence that Pullman was originally under Mellon family control, and that Mellon interests "continue to wield enormous influence." However, as was suggested in Chapter 2, there is no reason to assume that Morgan and Mellon influence could not have operated simultaneously.

3. This case was interesting, since in 1908 J. P. Morgan had refused to underwrite GM, thinking it a bad investment, and GM was forced to go to Lee, Higginson & Co. of Boston for financing. By 1915, after General Motors had proven itself viable, J. P. Morgan & Co. became interested (Carosso, 1970).

4. Allen's data include 125 industrials, 17 transports, 48 utilities, 10 retailers, 17 insurance companies, and 33 commercial banks. Bunting's data (those employed here) include 100 industrials, 25 transports, 10 insurance companies, 12 investment banks, and 20 commercial banks.

5. Centrifugality, a term from graph theory, was employed by Sonquist and Koenig (1976) as a measure of the exclusiveness of a clique. It is defined as the number of within-group interlocks divided by the total number of system interlocks among the corporations in a particular clique.

6. The directional network contained 6 cliques, 4 of which were led by banks, and 1 by an insurance company. The average size of 6.0 was primarily a result of the large size of the Citibank clique (20). The average size of the remaining 5 cliques was a mere 3.2. And the average density of the 6 groups (.183) was again primarily a result of the low density of the Citibank group. Although I am using the strong tie peak analysis for 1969, it is worthwhile to note the considerable alteration of the clique structure produced by the alternative criteria (see Appendix for a list of the cliques), especially in light of the criticisms of peak analysis in Chapter 4.

CHAPTER 7

THE INSTITUTIONALIZATION OF
INTERCORPORATE RELATIONS

Berle and Means (1968) believed that the separation of ownership from control had major consequences for the behavior of
large corporations. Later managerialists focused on changes in
class structure and political relations which supposedly resulted
from the dispersal of majority stockholdings. In this study I
have looked at one particular aspect of this issue: the consequences of stock dispersal for the structure of relations among
large corporations.[1] I have argued that in order to understand
corporate control, corporations must be viewed as elements of
an interorganizational system. I then presented a model of
relative influence based on a firm's centrality in the network of
interlocking directorates. The network was examined in three
general areas: the extent of its connectedness; the centrality of
particular corporations; and the existence and development of
cliques in the network.

The findings presented in the preceding chapters indicate that
the managerialist thesis of growing corporate independence is
partially accurate, but that its applicability is limited to a
relatively small time span under very specific conditions.
Between 1912, perhaps the height of unrestricted big business
activity in American history, and 1935, the midst of the Great
Depression, the connectivity of the network declined considerably. Interlocks in 1935 were less than one-half as frequent as in
1912. The density of the network was also cut in half. These
two developments suggest that at the time Berle and Means
were writing (the early 1930s), a major trend toward growing
corporate independence had been under way for nearly two

decades. However, after 1935, contrary to the claims of managerialists writing in the 1950s and 1960s, the trend toward declining corporate interdependence came to a halt. By 1969, at the height of the merger movement of the late 1960s, interlocking and network density were at levels 15 percent higher than in 1935. Even with a considerable decline in 1974 as the wave of mergers came to an end, connectivity remained slightly above the 1935 level.

Furthermore, despite the declining centrality of investment banks after 1919, the network remained dominated by commercial banks. Despite a declining number of interlocks and a declining number of outgoing interlocks, the relative centrality of commercial banks remained roughly equal during the entire 70-year period. Only in 1919 and 1964 did relative bank centrality decline significantly, but in both cases it increased in subsequent years. The managerialist claim that banks are no longer powerful in relation to nonfinancials clearly appears in need of modification.

And finally, the concept of an economy dominated by several distinct interest groups which dissolved over time has been called into question by our findings. The corporate system was so totally dominated by J. P. Morgan & Co. early in the century that it was not until 1935 that distinct cliques even emerged. And only by 1964 did groups clearly outside of both the Morgan and the New York spheres of influence appear. But, even then, the overlap among the groups was so extensive that to speak of distinct interest groups was a considerable exaggeration.

In all, fifteen hypotheses were employed to examine the managerialist thesis. Table 7.1 presents a summary of the findings. Of the fifteen managerialist hypotheses treated in this study, only three are clearly supported by the data. Two of these are related to the hierarchy within the system, which appears to have declined somewhat. The other, sending interlocks from financial to nonfinancial corporations, suggests a decline in direct control relations between financials and nonfinancials. These two findings combined suggest that the

TABLE 7.1   Results of Hypothesis Testing

Hypothesis	Supports Managerialist Thesis?
(I) *Connectivity*	
(1) Number of Interlocks	Partially
(2) Density	Partially
(3) Interlocked Position Ratio	Partially
(4) Reach	NO
(II) *Financial Centrality*	
(5) Financial-Nonfinancial Interlocks	Partially
(6) Centrality of Financials	NO
(7) Number of Financials among Most Central	Partially
(8) Proportion of Sending Interlocks	YES
(9) Directional/Nondirectional Centrality	NO
(10) Relative Stability	NO
(III) *Cliques*	
(11) Disintegration of Cliques	NO
(12) Distribution of Interlocking	YES
(13) Distribution of Centrality	YES
(14) Financial versus Geographical Cliques	NO
(15) Financials as Peaks	NO

phenomenon of direct, hierarchical bank *control* of industry has become less pronounced in recent years. However, as the other findings indicate, financials, banks in particular, remain in strategically located positions in the network.

It is worthwhile at this juncture to comment briefly on the implications of these findings for the decades-old debate over bank control of nonfinancial corporations. The debate generally falls into three categories. First is the managerialist position, which has been presented throughout this study. The managerialist argument suggests that, through their increasing ability to finance investment with retained earnings, nonfinancial corporations have gradually freed themselves from the dictates of financial corporations. A second position, termed "managerial Marxism," (Mintz, 1978) accepts the empirical arguments about management control and the decline of financial power put forth by managerialists, but denies that these changes have (1) altered corporate behavior from the traditional goal of profit maximization or (2) altered the class structure of advanced capitalist societies. Prominent among these theorists are Baran and Sweezy (1966), O'Connor (1968, 1972), and Miliband (1969). The work of Herman (1973, 1975, 1981) can also be placed within this perspective. Finally, the finance capital perspective, an outgrowth of the arguments of Hilferding (1981) and Lenin (1975), argues that financial institutions, through their control over investment capital and other sources of credit, effectively dominate most nonfinancial corporations. Among the recent proponents of this position are Fitch and Oppenheimer (1970) and Knowles (1973).

Based on the data presented here, none of the three positions appears to hold sway. As noted above, the managerialist position, including its cooptation model derivative, is called into question by the continued cohesiveness of the corporate network and the persistent centrality of financial institutions.[2] The managerial Marxist position corresponds with the cohesion of the network, but not with the continuing centrality of financials. Finally, the finance capital perspective, while supported by both the cohesion of the network and the centrality of financial institutions, is contradicted by the declining incidence of financial representation on the boards of nonfinancials. As pointed out in Chapter 5, direct control relations between financials and nonfinancials appear to have declined since the early 1900s.

In two recent works, Mintz and Schwartz (1980, forthcoming) have proposed a "finance hegemony" model. Other theorists, including Koenig (Sonquist and Koenig, 1976; Koenig et al., 1979), Domhoff (1979), and Useem (1980) have proposed a "class hegemony" model. The finance hegemony model differs from the finance capital position in two respects. First, it agrees with other theorists that dyadic control relations between individual financial and nonfinancial corporations are largely a thing of the past. Second, it locates the source of this trend in the growing inability of individual banks and other institutions to single-handedly finance corporate loans. Instead, large consortia, often numbering as many as 200 institutions, are necessary for major corporate financing schemes. As a result, large financial corporations now act increasingly as a group. While not actually involved in day-to-day decision making, they are able to set the guidelines within which corporate decisions are made.[3]

The class hegemony position is similar to that of the finance hegemony model in that it recognizes the critical role of banks in the center of the network. However, its emphasis is more tilted toward the fusion of financial and industrial capital rather than the distinctions between them. This fusion is exemplified by the multisector representation on bank boards, which are viewed as the centers of classwide leadership and influence. However, it is emphasized that these boards consist not only of bankers but also of leaders from major industries.

Both views fit our data better than either the traditional bank control model or the managerial Marxist position. In order to distinguish the two, one would have to examine the extent to which the same industries continue to be represented on bank boards over time. Since both models are attempts to describe the corporate system as it exists today, the data in this study would have to come from relatively recent, or even future years. If the banks continue to remain highly central while the industries represented on bank boards fluctuate over time, the finance hegemony model would be supported. If the represented industries remain stable, or if the central financials themselves fluctuate, the class model would be supported.

Thus, while both the finance hegemony and class hegemony views are well-supported by our findings, further research is necessary to untangle the relations between the models and the data. Still, our data suggest that, given their central location in the network, banks (and financials in general) are in positions to articulate the views and interests of the system as a whole. These positions give financial institutions a disproportionate share of influence in the network. That this influence may be translated into hegemony is an inference which calls for serious investigation.

Effects of the Clayton Act

As we have seen, the connectivity of the network declined significantly between 1912 and 1935, but not thereafter. Thus, to the extent that the managerialist thesis is accurate, it is accurate for a specific 20-year period. An examination of the sources of these changes is appropriate here.

Two crucial changes occurred after 1912. First, the Clayton Antitrust Act of 1914 outlawed interlocks between competing firms. In 1912, the 20 banks in our sample interlocked 124 times with one another. By 1919, they interlocked only 19 times. Second, the number of heavily interlocked individuals declined sharply. These two issues will be discussed separately.

The effect of legislation on interlocking is a crucial issue here, since it is possible that the decreased interlocking between 1912 and 1919 was primarily a result of the Clayton Act rather than indicative of actual changes in intercorporate relations. For example, after the Armstrong Investigation of 1905, interlocks involving insurance companies were cut in half (see Chapter 5). This investigation, undertaken during a period of mounting public protest against big business, revealed that insurance companies held major stockholdings in banks, and legislation was promptly passed requiring these companies to dispose of their bank holdings (Brandeis, 1914).

The sharp decline of insurance company interlocking between 1904 and 1912 appears to have been a consequence of this incident. However, the Pujo Committee (1913) revealed that investment banks, in particular J. P. Morgan & Co., were the main controllers of the insurance companies. "Within five years all of these stocks, so far as distributed by the insurance companies, . . . found their way into the hands of the men who virtually controlled or were identified with the management of the insurance companies or of their close allies or associates" (quoted in Brandeis, 1914: 12). In other words, the legislation was, to quote Sobel (1965: 185), "promptly circumvented."

Was the Clayton Act circumvented as well? This question is surprisingly difficult to answer. Although the sharpest decline between 1912 and 1919 was in bank horizontal interlocks (124 to 19), interlocks between banks and railroads (237 to 125) and banks and industrials (295 to 200) also declined considerably. Furthermore, the decline in interlocking that began after 1912 continued between 1912 and 1935. The 30.4 percent decline in the 16-year 1919-1935 period was not as sharp as the 32.9 percent drop in the 7-year 1912-1919 period, but it did suggest that what began around 1912 was a trend which would have occurred irrespective of the Clayton Act.

One way to measure this more systematically with the interlock data available to us is to determine the frequency with which indirect links through third parties were created after a direct link was broken. To do this, I took a random sample of 200 intercorporate links from 1912 and compared them in 1919. Because some firms from 1912 were no longer in the 1919 data set, a final sample of 145 links emerged. Among the 145 ties in 1912, only 63 (43 percent) remained directly linked in 1919. However, 61 of the 82 broken ties remained linked indirectly. The sample was then divided into two groups, those to which the Clayton Act was in some way directed and those which were not so designated. In both groups (n = 95 and n = 50, respectively) roughly the same proportion were broken during this period (57 percent to 52 percent), indicating that interlocking probably would have declined regardless of the Clayton Act. But there was a higher rate of indirect interlocking within the former group (45 percent to 34 percent), suggesting that there may have been some tendency to establish second-order interlocks to circumvent the Clayton Act.

To further answer this question, I conducted a detailed examination of all bank horizontal ties severed between 1912 and 1919. Of the 30 links which were in the sample in both years, 25 were broken between 1912 and 1919. Of these 25, 24 were linked indirectly in 1919. There was a total of 96 indirect bank links in 1919, 59 of which remained from 1912, and 37 of which were newly established in 1919. If second-order interlocks were indeed mechanisms for continued links among banks, then these 37 newly added ties should be the focus of our concern. Furthermore, we should be particularly concerned with situations in which bank representatives sit on the boards of a third corporation. This is most likely to be indicative of deliberate interlocking by the banks. The 59 maintained second-order links will be used as a control group.

Among the 37 new second-order bank ties, only 8 (22 percent) involved representatives from both banks. This is slightly higher than the proportion among the 59 maintained second-order links (10, or 17 percent) but low enough to suggest that most new indirect links were not directly tied to the Clayton Act. Still, *not one* of these 37 links involved both banks as receivers, compared with 9 of the 59 maintained links. And the overall direction of interlocking differed between new and maintained links. The 59 maintained links accounted for 190 total interlocks. Of these 190, 87 (46 percent) were weak ties. Of the 103 strong ties, only 48 (47 percent) involved banks sending to nonbanks. The 37 newly added links accounted for 98 interlocks, 55 of which (56 percent) were weak ties. But, of the 43 newly added strong ties, 35 (81 percent) were bank sending interlocks. Since only 56 percent of all directional bank interlocks with nonfinancials in 1919 were sending interlocks, this further suggests that many newly established second-order ties may have been created to circumvent the Clayton Act. Nevertheless, it should be remembered that only 21 percent of the newly added links involved representatives of both banks. These findings suggest that the Clayton Act did directly affect interlocking and that it was circumvented to some extent. But they do *not* indicate that the law was the principal cause of the decline in interlocks after 1912. To find this cause, we must look elsewhere.

Multiple Interlocking Among Individuals

The place to look, I would argue, is in the changing nature of the economy from one dominated by individuals to one dominated by institutions. Prior to the Clayton Act, a relatively small group of capitalists effectively dominated the economy. A reading of American corporate history suggests that these individuals were as important as the corporations they represented. J. P. Morgan & Co. was identified with J. P. Morgan, First

National Bank with George F. Baker, Standard Oil with John D. and William Rockefeller, and National City Bank with James Stillman. While control over these particular corporations may have served as the basis of their power, these people had a number of other interests as well. In terms of directorships, 24 individuals held 6 or more seats in 1904, and 27 held as many in 1912. The individuals with the highest number of directorships were precisely those considered most powerful at the time: Morgan (8 seats in 1904), Baker (11), Stillman (13), Schiff (7), Harriman (11), W. Rockefeller (9).[4]

By 1912, many of these people had either died (Harriman), retired (John D. Rockefeller), or curtailed their activities (Schiff, Morgan). For example, in 1904 J. P. Morgan held eight directorships while his son, J. P. Morgan, Jr., held only one, his position at the Morgan bank. By 1912, Morgan, Sr., held only six positions, while Morgan, Jr., held five.

By 1919, the character of the system had changed as well. From 27 individuals with 6 or more directorships accounting for 213 positions in 1912, only 14 individuals held 6 or more directorships in 1919, accounting for 100 positions. By 1935, only 3 individuals held 6 or more directorships, accounting for just 19 positions. These changes are evident from an impressionistic reading of historical accounts of the period. Discussions of the activities of Morgan, Stillman, and Schiff are replaced by discussions of the House of Morgan, National City Bank, and Kuhn, Loeb & Co. The leading individuals of the 1919-1935 period, Wiggin, Stotesbury, Mitchell, as well as J. P. Morgan, Jr., though important and influential, are a far cry from the capitalists of the previous generation.

While this finding is consistent and corresponds with theories of the managerial revolution, postindustrial society, and the technostructure, to say that it demonstrates the "decomposition of capital" or the growth of managerial autonomy is not consistent with our findings on interorganizational connections. In short, the fact that we no longer have individuals with the power of J. P. Morgan may indicate little about the decline in intercorporate cohesion and interdependence.

A comparison of the fate of the Morgan and Harriman properties serves to illustrate this. By 1907, Edward H. Harriman had developed interests in 27 railroads, plus Guaranty Trust and Equitable Life Assurance (Corey, 1930: 352). However, in the face of public and governmental opposition, Harriman was unable to consolidate his power. "Moreover," as Corey (1930: 352) points out, "Harriman was incapable of institutionalizing his system, as Morgan did: everything, with him, seemed to require the personal touch. . . . He died in 1909, and the Harriman system collapsed." Morgan, on the other hand, was able to avoid a similar fate precisely because he did institutionalize his system. Long after his death, J. P. Morgan & Co. representatives remained on the boards of U.S. Steel, General Electric, International Harvester, and others, as well as on the boards of Bankers Trust and Guaranty Trust. Firms not directly under the J. P. Morgan & Co. domain were covered by Bankers and Guaranty, and Mutual and New York Life Insurance Companies.[5] In Corey's (1930: 415) words:

> Morgan's death . . . produced no effect on the system of centralization nor in the House of Morgan, creating scarcely a ripple. J. Pierpont Morgan, Jr., . . . succeeded his father and the House of Morgan functioned smoothly.

By 1935, the chairmanship of J. P. Morgan & Co. had passed to George P. Whitney, but the House of Morgan maintained its influence (Josephson, 1972).

There were other examples as well.

> Although James Stillman retired from active control of the National City Bank, his successor, Frank A. Vanderlip, continued its aggressive policy of expansion, extending the Bank's control of trust companies and increasing its affiliations with large institutions in other cities [Corey, 1930: 351].

Once the system of connections was established, it was no longer necessary for Morgan, Stillman, or Rockefeller to preside over particular corporations. Thus, the system changed from one dominated by a few individuals to one dominated by specific institutions. The decline of corporate interlocking between 1912 and 1935 was therefore to a great extent a result of the decline of individual domination of the system. But it represented the crystallization of the system of institutionalized intercorporate relations. The maintenance of a solidified, connected network suggested a continuation in the character of those relations: overlapping, interdependent, and ultimately unified.

This process, which can be referred to as the institutionalization of intercorporate relations, represents the culmination of a 50-year period of rapid industrialization and concentration of capital in the United States, which peaked between 1890 and 1912. It was during this period that the system of competitive capitalism gave way to a new form of capitalism. This system has been referred to as financial capitalism (Hilferding, Lenin), monopoly capitalism (Baran and Sweezy), corporate capitalism (Domhoff), and late capitalism (Mandel). But regardless of what it is designated, virtually all observers agree that the system that emerged after World War I had a qualitatively different character from the economy of pre-Civil War days.

Because this was a unique era in American history, it might be difficult or even unwise to draw generalizations from it. However, an interesting analogy can be made between the institutionalization process described here and Weber's (1968) concept of the routinization of charisma.

Weber's concept of charisma was part of his analysis of the forms of legitimate domination in a society.[6] According to Weber, every system of domination attempts to establish and cultivate a belief in its legitimacy. There are three general types of legitimate authority: legal, traditional, and charismatic. Legal authority rests on "a belief in the legality of enacted rules and the right of those elevated to authority under such rules to issue commands" (Weber, 1968: 215). Contemporary western parliamentary democracies are examples of legal authority. Weber's well-known discussion of bureaucracy is also based on this concept. Traditional authority rests on "an established belief in the sanctity of immemorial traditions and the legitimacy of those exercising authority under them" (p. 215). Feudal and patriarchal societies were examples of this type of authority. Charismatic authority rests on "devotion to the exceptional sanctity, heroism, or exemplary character of an individual person, and of the normative patterns or order revealed or ordained by him" (p. 215). Charismatic leaders are capable of mobilizing masses of people to their support. However, because of what Weber believed was its irrational nature, this form of domination is difficult to administer in a stable manner. Thus, in a social movement led by a charismatic figure, the assumption of power may necessitate major changes in the style of leadership. As Weber (1968: 246) put it:

> In its pure form charismatic authority has a character specifically foreign to everyday routine structures. . . . If this is not to remain a purely transitory phenomenon, but to take on the character of a permanent relationship, a "community" of disciples or followers or a party organization . . . it is necessary for the character of charismatic authority to become radically changed. . . . It cannot remain stable, but becomes either traditionalized or rationalized, or a combination of both.

The problem of leadership succession becomes particularly important, for now the "disciples" have a vested interest in "continuing . . . in such a way that both from an ideal and a material point of view, their own position is put on a stable everyday basis" (Weber, 1968: 246).

Let us assume for the moment that the individual leaders of the major corporations discussed above (Morgan, Rockefeller, Stillman, Baker, and others) were charismatic leaders within the corporations or corporate empires which they controlled. Their underlings may be treated as "disciples." In J. P. Morgan & Co., First National Bank, and Standard Oil, leadership passed from Morgan, Baker, and Rockefeller to their sons, J. P. Morgan, Jr., George F. Baker, Jr., and John D. Rockefeller, Jr. This corresponds with Weber's charisma "transmitted by heredity." In the National City Bank, James Stillman, who had no sons, passed the leadership on to Frank A. Vanderlip, National City president and an advisor to Stillman. Vanderlip represented an example of transmission by "designation on the part of the original charismatic leader" (Weber, 1968: 247). In the case of transmission via heredity, Weber (1968: 248) stresses that

> recognition is no longer paid to the charismatic qualities of the individual, but to the legitimacy of the position he has acquired by hereditary succession. . . . Personal charisma may be totally absent.

In the case of succession by designation, "legitimacy is *acquired* through the act of designation" (Weber, 1968: 247; emphasis in original), again a process which may have nothing to do with the successor's personal qualities.

Thus, according to Weber's scheme, the early twentieth century in the United States was characterized by several examples of charismatic leadership in which the routinization process accelerated as the leaders were succeeded. The authority of the new leaders was based not on their own charismatic personal qualities but on their institutional positions. If we raise the analysis to the level of the system as a whole, it suggests an example of a few charismatic figures who ushered the society through a period of rapid transformation and established a cohesive system of intercorporate relations. When the leaders died or retired, power passed to their sons or to handpicked successors, who ruled not on the basis of their unique personal qualities but on the foundations established by their predecessors. What were the conditions which made it possible for certain individuals to attain such power? The conjecture from this study is that it is likely to occur when an older form of society gives way and a vacuum is created. The vacuum is filled by those who have the initiative, and more importantly, access to resources which enable them to affect changes and create new structures. In the turn of the century United States, Morgan, Rockefeller, and others had access to capital, which enabled them to lay the foundations for the system of intercorporate relations which has continued to the present day.[7]

Finally, and it is important to stress this point, the ascendence of a more bureaucratic form of corporate organization should not be confused with the transcendence of capitalism as a system. Corporations continued to profit maximize, to respond to the market, and to act in relation to one another. What the institutionalization process wrought was a formal structure to the new form of capitalism, a structure based on stable relations among major corporations rather than on the machinations of a few individuals.

This does not mean that individual entrepreneurs have entirely disappeared. On the contrary, tycoons such as the Insulls and Van Sweringens in the 1920s and 1930s, Robert Young in the 1940s and 1950s, James Ling and Howard Hughes in the 1960s, and the Hunts in the 1970s continue to operate, amassing fabulous sums of wealth by manipulating corporations, the stock market, and/or the futures markets. But, unlike the great capitalists of an earlier age, these entrepreneurs exist on the fringes of the system. Rather than directing corporate activity from the pillars of the New York financial district, these individuals are now seen as the protagonists in a battle with the faceless Wall Street "establishment."[8] This establishment now consists of such giants as First National City Bank, Morgan Guaranty Trust, Chase Manhattan Bank, Manufacturers Hanover Trust, Chemical Bank, and Bankers Trust in New York, and the major banks in places such as Chicago, Pittsburgh, and California. Among the heads of these banks, only David Rockefeller of Chase (recently retired) is easily identifiable, but his individual power, though extensive, is nowhere near that of J. P. Morgan at the turn of the century. To quote Josephson (1972: 286):

> The old power centers are there in Wall Street, holding their strategic positions and interlocking corporate controls; yet they no longer rule through that tight "community of interests" J. P. Morgan once fashioned.

Nevertheless,

> when there is a crisis, when money is lost, and the need of liquid capital becomes urgent, then we find that the great trust companies,

insurance companies, investment bankers, and mutual funds . . . may move in on the situation with great speed, oust the management, and replace it. . . . It is well never to underestimate the power of the bankers [p. 287].[9]

The banks remain in the center of the corporate network, perhaps not as dominant as in the first decade of this century, but more influential than any other element in the system.

Conclusion

The managerialist thesis pointed to a number of actual changes taking place in American society in the early part of the century. Large family stockholdings were to a considerable extent dispersed. The influence of a few individuals declined. And, corresponding to these changes, the density of the network of interlocking directorates decreased. Where the managerialists erred was in describing what replaced the previous situation.

First, large family stockholdings have to a great extent been replaced by institutional stockholdings. The TNEC report revealed that, while bank stockholdings existed in the 1930s, they were relatively small. By the 1960s, the Patman report demonstrated the existence of large and extensive holdings by bank trust departments. Second, although the age of J. P. Morgan and John D. Rockefeller came to an end, the influence of the institutions they had established remained. Many of the most central corporations of the early 1900s remain among the most central into the 1970s. Third, the system of intercorporate ties has remained intact, long after Morgan and Rockefeller passed from the scene. While the corporations are not as tightly connected in recent years as they were in the pre-1935 era, they remain linked nonetheless, more strongly connected in the 1960s and 1970s than in 1935.

What are the implications of these findings for theories of social class in the United States? Is there a cohesive capitalist class, or at least a unified corporate elite? The findings presented in this study are not sufficient to answer these questions. However, they do lend themselves to some suggestions. First, if we accept the fact that there was any kind of "community of interest" early in the century, as virtually all historical accounts indicate, then there is no evidence that this community of interest has dissolved. Over 80 percent of our 167-corporation network remains completely interconnected into the 1970s, at distances no greater than those of the 1904-1912 period. Starting at the center of the network, 91 percent of all corporations in 1969 and 85 percent in 1974 are within three steps, compared with 91 percent in 1904 and 82 percent in 1912. In 1969, there were 987 interlocked board positions within our sample, compared with 974 in 1912.

Second, there is nothing random about the character of the structure. A small group of New York financial institutions dominates the network in the 1964-1974 period as in 1904 and 1912. As the importance of railroads declines and that of industrials increases, their positions in the network do likewise. When this interlock evidence is combined with data on the magnitude of institutional stockholdings by major financial institutions (for example, see Kotz, 1978; Patman Committee, 1968), it is apparent that the interlock network provides a valid portrait of intercorporate connectedness and influence.

Third, there is little indication of separate, clearly distinct interest groups in which conflict forms the basis of their interrelations. Instead, we see some clustering, but far more overlapping and blurring of distinctions among the groups that do exist. In short, given the findings of this study, it is difficult to accept Dahrendorf's (1959: 47) observation of the corporate system as a group of "partly agreed, partly competing, and partly simply different groups." Rather, we appear to have a system of interdependent, partly competing, but generally cohesive groups, with a unity of interest far deeper than whatever conflicts over policy may exist.

A copious and growing literature has demonstrated that leaders of major corporations interlock not only through board memberships but also through memberships in social clubs, cultural, and governmental decision-making bodies (Domhoff, 1967; Freitag, 1975; Mintz, 1975; Soref, 1976; Koenig et al., 1979; Ratcliff et al., 1979; Useem, 1979; Salzman and Domhoff, 1980).[10] This indicates to some that the United States has a dominant social class which exists above and beyond peoples' positions within particular corporations, and that the corporations themselves may be but tools for the more general accumulation of capital by major capitalist families (Zeitlin, 1974). This may or may not be true, but there is no reason that it must be a necessary condition for the existence of a cohesive capitalist class. The basic economic institution in contemporary capitalist society is the large corporation. If these corporations are themselves intertwined into a coherent and cohesive system, then it may be irrelevant whether the ties are based on family control, historical tradition, or contemporary necessity. Of course, the ability to demonstrate the family basis of this institutional control would certainly lend further credence to the claim that there is an active capitalist class in American society. My point is that even if managerialists are correct that corporations are run by faceless bureaucrats from all segments of society, this would in no way disprove the existence of a cohesive corporate elite. After J. P. Morgan's death, his system of institutional control remained. If the Rockefellers suddenly disappeared, would the Chase Manhattan Bank slip into oblivion?

Finally, there is the broader issue of the relation between corporations and the government. Again, the data presented here do not touch directly on this topic, but they are relevant nonetheless. When the modern pluralist school in political sociology emerged, its leaders conceded that elites make most of the major decisions in American society (Schumpeter, 1942; Rose, 1967; Prewitt and Stone, 1973; Ricci, 1971), but argued that these elites had in recent years become essentially divided, with a plurality of interests. In fact, they argued, it was precisely these divisions that enabled industrialized western societies to maintain their democratic traditions. The presence of an essentially unified corporate elite does not prove that business controls government, as some claim. But if democracy in our society depends on a divided elite, and if that elite is not essentially divided, then what does this say about the viability of the democracy? Sociologists are only beginning to take this question seriously. Given its significance, this attention is long overdue.

NOTES

1. This study has concerned itself with American corporations only. A recent article by Fennema and Schijf (1979) provided a thorough review of a number of European interlock studies. Mokken and Stokman (1979) have begun a study of interlocking across national boundaries. The rise of multinational corporations and the growing internationalization of the world economy suggests that comparative and international interlock research will become increasingly important in the future.

2. Although the cooptation model may be consistent with the continued cohesion of the network, the persistent centrality of financials gives a hierarchy and coherence to the structure incommensurate with managerial autonomy. Our findings are more consistent with the modified resource dependence model discussed in Chapters 2 and 4.

3. Here Mintz and Schwartz borrow Gramsci's (1971) concept of "ideological hegemony" (see also Sallach, 1974).

4. See Allen (1935) and Bunting and Barbour (1971) for a discussion of these individuals. Most of the historical sources cited earlier in this study contain detailed descriptions of their activities.

5. Notice, for example, how J. P. Morgan & Co. maintains its high centrality despite a relatively small number of interlocks.

6. In the earlier translations of Weber by Talcott Parsons, the term *Herrschaft* was translated as "authority." In the edition edited by Roth and Wittich employed here, it is defined as "domination." However, in a footnote, the editors point out that "Weber placed the term *'Authoritat'* in quotation marks and parentheses behind *'Herrschaft,'* referring to an alternative colloquial term" (Weber, 1968: 299). Hence, in *Economy and Society*, the terms *domination* and *authority* are used interchangeably. I shall follow this procedure here.

7. Of course, not all of these capitalists were capable of mobilizing masses of people to their support. In fact, in most cases, the only masses mobilized by these leaders were members of populist and progressive movements who were mobilized *against* them. Still, in the business world, the names of Morgan and Rockefeller carried tremendous prestige. And Morgan in particular possessed many qualities which might be referred to as charismatic. See the discussion of how Morgan single-handedly ended the panic of 1907 in Sobel (1965: 190-198).

8. Matthew Josephson's *The Money Lords* (1972) provides a fascinating account of several battles between these outsiders and the Wall Street hierarchy during the 1920-1970 period. In recent years, the exploits of Saul P. Steinberg provide an intriguing example. Steinberg, head of Reliance Group (formerly Leasco), became famous in 1969 when he unsuccessfully attempted to acquire Chemical Bank. Within two weeks of his plan becoming known, Leasco's institutional stockholders (which included most of the major New York banks) "dumped" their stock, causing the price to drop from $140 to $106 per share, thus ending the bid (Glasberg, 1981). In what has become one of the most oft-quoted statements in the annals of corporate research, Steinberg moaned, "I always knew there was an Establishment. I just used to think I was part of it" (*Business Week*, 1970: 54).

9. For a number of examples of this, see Business Week (1970), Fitch and Oppenheimer (1970), Josephson (1972), and Mintz and Schwartz (1980), as well as Chapter 2 above. A recent example is the case of International Harvester, which was forced to request its bankers to restructure its finances (*Business Week*, June 22, 1981: 66-72).

10. Dunn (1980) has documented the existence of "family offices" through which a number of capitalist families manage their business and social affairs.

APPENDIX

Cliques According to Alternative Criteria, 1935-1974

1935 (Directional)

Northwestern Mutual Life
 (Milwaukee)
Southern Railway (Richmond)
Allis-Chalmers (Milwaukee)

(4) Climax Molybdenum
 (New York)
American Metal Climax
 (New York)
C. M. Loeb & Co. (New York)

(5) Blyth & Co. (San Francisco)
Crown Zellerbach
 (San Francisco)

(6) Wheeling Steel (Wheeling)
Seaboard Air Line (Richmond)

1964 (Directional)

(1) Mellon National Bank[a]
 (Pittsburgh)
Gulf Oil (Pittsburgh)
U.S. Steel (New York)
Aluminum Co. of America
 (Pittsburgh)
Pennsylvania R.R.
 (Philadelphia)
Chrysler (Detroit)
Jones & Laughlin Steel
 (Pittsburgh)
Pittsburgh Plate Glass
 (Pittsburgh)
Westinghouse (Pittsburgh)

(2) Brown Brothers, Harriman
 & Co. (New York)
Prudential Insurance
 (New York)

(3) New York Central (Albany)
Smith, Barney, & Co.
 (New York)

(4) National Bank of Detroit
 (Detroit)
Dow Chemical (Detroit)
National Steel (Pittsburgh)

(5) Cleveland Trust (Cleveland)
Firestone Tire & Rubber
 (Akron)

1964 (Directional)

---

(6) Burlington Industries
     (Greensboro)
    R. J. Reynolds Tobacco
     (Winston-Salem)

1969 (Directional)

---

(1) First National City Bank
     (New York)
    Olin Mathieson Chemical
     (Stamford)
    Chemical Bank (New York)
    United Aircraft (Hartford)
    NCR (Dayton)
    Monsanto (St. Louis)
    Xerox (Rochester)
    DuPont (Wilmington)
    Borden (New York)
    ITT (New York)
    B. F. Goodrich (New York)
    Ford Motor (Detroit)
    McDonnell-Douglas (St. Louis)
    Western Electric (New York)
    Massachusetts Mutual Life
     (Springfield)
    General Dynamics (New York)
    Firestone Tire & Rubber
     (Akron)
    E. F. Hutton (New York)
    Missouri Pacific (St. Louis)

(2) Morgan Guaranty Trust
     (New York)
    Control Data (Minneapolis)
    Santa Fe Industries (Chicago)

(3) Mellon National Bank
     (Pittsburgh)
    PPG Industries (Pittsburgh)
    Gulf Oil (Pittsburgh)

(4) Charter NY Corp. (New York)
    General Telephone
     & Electronics (New York)
    Tenneco (Wilmington)

(5) John Hancock Mutual Life
     (Boston)
    First National Bank (Boston)
    Eastern Airlines (New York)

1969 (Directional)

(6) National Steel (Pittsburgh)
     National Bank of Detroit
        (Detroit)
     Dow Chemical (New York)
     Burroughs (Detroit)

1974 (Strong Tie)

(1) Morgan Guaranty Trust[b]
        (New York)
     Aetna Life (Hartford)
     Bethlehem Steel (Bethlehem)
     U.S. Steel (New York)
     Southern Railway (Richmond)
     General Motors (Detroit)
     New York Life (New York)
     Singer Mfg. (New York)
     Exxon (New York)
     Santa Fe Industries (Chicago)
     Proctor & Gamble (Cincinnati)
     General Electric (New York)
     Eastman Kodak (Rochester)
     Cities Service (New York)
     Western Electric (New York)
     Champion International
        (Toledo)
     Coca-Cola Co. (Atlanta)
     IBM (Armonk, New York)

(2) Bankers Trust (New York)
     American Can (New York)

(3) Continental Illinois Trust
        (Chicago)
     Chicago, Milwaukee, &
     St. Paul (Chicago)
     Illinois Central Industries
        (Chicago)
     Lykes-Youngstown
        (Youngstown)

(4) Dow Chemical (Detroit)
     Missouri Pacific (St. Louis)

a. Only clique members directly linked with Mellon are listed here.
b. Only clique members directly linked with Morgan are listed here.

REFERENCES

Alba, Richard D. (1973) "A graph-theoretic definition of a sociometric clique." Journal of Mathematical Sociology 3: 113-126.

Aldrich, Howard E. (1979) Organizations and Environments. Englewood Cliffs, NJ: Prentice-Hall.

Allen, Frederick Lewis (1935) The Lords of Creation. New York: Harper & Row.

Allen, Michael P. (1978) "Economic interest groups and the corporate elite structure." Social Science Quarterly 58: 597-615.

––– (1974) "The structure of interorganizational elite cooptation." American Sociological Review 39: 393-406.

Arabie, Phipps and Scott A. Boorman (1977) "Constructing blockmodels: how and why." Harvard-Yale Preprints in Mathematical Sociology 3.

Baran, Paul A. and Paul M. Sweezy (1966) Monopoly Capital. New York: Monthly Review Press.

Bass, B. M. (1949) "An analysis of the leaderless group discussion." Journal of Abnormal and Social Psychology 33: 527-533.

Bauer, Douglas (1981) "Why big business is firing the boss." New York Times Magazine (March 8): 22-25, 79-91.

Baumol, William J. (1959) Business Behavior, Value, and Growth. New York: Macmillan.

Bavelas, Alex (1950) "Communication patterns in task-oriented groups." Journal of the Acoustical Society of America 57: 271-282.

Bearden, James, William Atwood, Peter Freitag, Carol Hendricks, Beth Mintz, and Michael Schwartz (1975) "The nature and extent of bank centrality in corporate networks." Presented at the annual meeting of the American Sociological Association, San Francisco.

Beck, E. M., Patrick M. Horan, and Charles M. Tolbert II (1981) "Industrial segmentation and labor market discrimination." Social Problems 28: 113-130.

Bell, Daniel (1973) The Coming of Post-Industrial Society. New York: Basic Books.

––– (1960) The End of Ideology. New York: Collier.

Benson, J. Kenneth (1977) Organizational Analysis: Critique and Innovation. Beverly Hills, CA: Sage.

Berle, Adolf A. (1959a) "Forward," in Edward S. Mason (ed.) The Corporation in Modern Society. Cambridge, MA: Harvard University Press.

––– (1959b) Power Without Property. New York: Harcourt Brace Jovanovich.

––– (1954) The 20th Century Capitalist Revolution. New York: Harcourt Brace Jovanovich.

––– and Gardiner C. Means (1968) The Modern Corporation and Private Property. New York: Harcourt Brace Jovanovich. (Originally published in 1932.)

Blair, John M. (1976) The Control of Oil. New York: Random House.

Blau, Peter M. and Otis Dudley Duncan (1967) The American Occupational Structure. New York: John Wiley.

Blumberg, Phillip I. (1975) The Megacorporation in American Society: The Scope of Corporate Power. Englewood Cliffs, NJ: Prentice-Hall.

Bonacich, Phillip (1972a) "Technique for analyzing overlapping memberships," in Herbert Costner (ed.) Sociological Methodology. San Francisco: Jossey-Bass.

––– (1972b) "Factoring and weighting approaches to status scores and clique identification." Journal of Mathematical Sociology 2: 113-120.

Brandeis, Louis (1914) Other Peoples' Money. New York: Frederick A. Stokes.

Braverman, Harry (1974) Labor and Monopoly Capital. New York: Monthly Review Press.

Breiger, Ronald L., Scott A. Boorman, and Phipps Arabie (1975) "An algorithm for clustering relational data with applications to social network analysis and comparison with multidimensional scaling." Journal of Mathematical Psychology 12: 328-383.

Bullock, Charles J. (1903) "The concentration of banking interests in the United States." Atlantic Monthly 92: 182-192.

Bunting, David (1979) "Efficiency, equity, and the evolution of big business." Presented at the annual meeting of the Western Economic Association, Las Vegas.

––– (1977) "Corporate interlocking: Part IV–A new look at interlocks and legislation." Directors and Boards 1 (Winter): 39-47.

––– (1976a) "Corporate interlocking: Part III–Interlocks and return on investment." Directors and Boards 1 (Fall): 4-11.

––– (1976b) "Corporate interlocking: Part II–The modern money trust." Directors and Boards 1 (Summer): 27-37.

––– and Jeffrey Barbour (1971) "Interlocking directorates in large American corporations, 1896-1964." Business History Review 45: 317-335.

Burch, Philip H., Jr. (1972) The Managerial Revolution Reassessed. Lexington, MA: D. C. Heath.

Burnham, James (1941) The Managerial Revolution. New York: John Day.

Burt, Ronald S. (1979) "A structural theory of interlocking directorates." Social Networks 1: 415-435.

––– Kenneth P. Christman, and Harold Kilburn, Jr. (1980) "Testing a structural theory of corporate cooptation: interorganizational directorate ties as a strategy for avoiding market constraints on profits." American Sociological Review 45: 821-841.

Business Week (1970) "Why the big traders worry industry," July 25: 53-61.

Carosso, Vincent P. (1970) Investment Banking in America. Cambridge, MA: Harvard University Press.

Chandler, Alfred D. (1977) The Visible Hand. Cambridge, MA: Harvard University Press.

Cochran, Thomas C. and William Miller (1961) The Age of Enterprise. New York: Harper & Row. (Originally published in 1942.)

Collier, Peter and David Horowitz (1976) The Rockefellers: An American Dynasty. New York: Holt, Rinehart & Winston.

Corey, Lewis (1930) The House of Morgan. New York: G. Howard Watt.

Cyert, Richard M. and James G. March (1963) A Behavioral Theory of the Firm. Englewood Cliffs, NJ: Prentice-Hall.

Daggett, S. (1908) Railroad Reorganization. Boston: Houghton Mifflin.

Dahl, Robert A. (1970) After the Revolution? New Haven, CT: Yale University Press.

Dahrendorf, Ralf (1959) Class and Class Conflict in Industrial Society. Stanford, CA: Stanford University Press.

Domhoff, G. William (1980) Power Structure Research. Beverly Hills, CA: Sage.

——— (1979) The Powers That Be. New York: Vintage.

——— (1967) Who Rules America? Englewood Cliffs, NJ: Prentice-Hall.

Dooley, Peter C. (1969) "The interlocking directorate." American Economic Review 59: 314-323.

Dunn, Marvin G. (1980) "The family office: coordinating mechanism of the ruling class," in G. William Domhoff (ed.) Power Structure Research. Beverly Hills, CA: Sage.

Durkheim, Emile (1933) The Division of Labor in Society. New York: Free Press. (Originally published in 1893.)

Elias, Christopher (1973) The Dollar Barons. New York: Macmillan.

Federal Trade Commission (1951) Report on Interlocking Directorates. Washington, DC: Government Printing Office.

Fennema, Meindert and Huibert Schijf (1979) "Analyzing interlocking directorates: theory and method." Social Networks 1: 297-332.

Fitch, Robert and Mary Oppenheimer (1970) "Who rules the corporations?" Socialist Revolution, Parts 1-3, 1 (4): 73-108; 1 (5): 61-114; 1 (6): 33-94.

Freitag, Peter (1975) "The cabinet and big business: a study of interlocks." Social Problems 23: 137-152.

Galaskiewicz, Joseph (1979) Exchange Networks and Community Politics. Beverly Hills, CA: Sage.

Galbraith, John Kenneth (1967) The New Industrial State. New York: New American Library.

Glasberg, Davita Silfen (1981) "The significance of corporate board interlocks: the case of Leasco Corp. vs. Chemical Bank." Presented at the annual meeting of the American Sociological Association, Toronto, August.

Gramsci, Antonio (1971) Selections from the Prison Notebooks (Quentin Hoare and Geoffrey Nowell Smith, eds. and trans.). New York: International.

Granovetter, Mark S. (1973) "The strength of weak ties." American Journal of Sociology 78: 1360-1379.

Herman, Edward S. (1981) Corporate Control, Corporate Power. New York: Cambridge University Press.

——— (1975) Conflicts of Interest: Commercial Bank Trust Departments. New York: Twentieth Century Fund.

——— (1973) "Do bankers control corporations?" Monthly Review 25: 12-29.

Hilferding, Rudolf (1981) Finance Capital. Boston: Routledge & Kegan Paul. (Originally published in German in 1910.)

Homans, George C. (1950) The Human Group. New York: Harcourt Brace Jovanovich.

Hopkins, Terence K. (1964) The Exercise of Influence in Small Groups. Totawa, NJ: Bedminster.

Horan, Patrick M. (1978) "Is status attainment research atheoretical?" American Sociological Review 43: 334-341.

Hubbell, C. H. (1965) "An input-output approach to clique identification." Sociometry 28: 377-399.

Hunter, Floyd (1953) Community Power Structure. Chapel Hill: University of North Carolina Press.

Josephson, Matthew (1972) The Money Lords. New York: New American Library.
——— (1934) The Robber Barons. New York: Harcourt Brace Jovanovich.
Kamerschen, David R. (1968) "The influence of ownership and control on profit rates." American Economic Review 58: 432-447.
Kaysen, Carl (1957) "The social significance of the modern corporation." American Economic Review 47: 311-319.
Keller, Morton (1963) Life Insurance Enterprise. Cambridge, MA: Harvard University Press.
Keys, C. M. (1910) "The building of a money trust." World's Work 19: 12618-12625.
Knowles, James C. (1973) "The Rockefeller Financial Group." Warner Modular Publications, Module 343.
Koenig, Thomas, Robert Gogel, and John Sonquist (1979) "Models of the significance of interlocking corporate directorates." American Journal of Economics and Sociology 38: 173-186.
Kotz, David M. (1979) "The significance of bank control over large corporations." Journal of Economic Issues 13: 407-426.
——— (1978) Bank Control of Large Corporations in the United States. Berkeley: University of California Press.
Larner, Robert J. (1970) Management Control and the Large Corporation. New York: Dunellen.
Laumann, Edward O. and Franz U. Pappi (1976) Networks of Collective Action: A Perspective on Community Influence Systems. New York: Academic.
Leavitt, Harold J. (1951) "Some effects of certain communications patterns on group performance." Journal of Abnormal and Social Psychology 46: 38-50.
Lenin, V. I. (1975) Imperialism: The Highest Stage of Capitalism. Peking: Foreign Language Press. (Originally published in 1917.)
Levine, Joel (1977) "The theory of bank control: comment on Mariolis' test of the theory." Social Science Quarterly 58: 506-510.
——— (1972) "The sphere of influence." American Sociological Review 37: 14-27.
Li, Jerome C. R. (1964) Statistical Inference: I. Ann Arbor, MI: Edwards Brothers.
Lintner, John (1959) "The financing of corporations," in Edward S. Mason (ed.) The Corporation in Modern Society. Cambridge, MA: Harvard University Press.
Lipset, Seymour Martin and William Schneider (1973) "Political sociology," in Neil J. Smelser (ed.) Sociology. New York: John Wiley.
Lorrain, Francois and Harrison C. White (1971) "Structural equivalence of individuals in social networks." Journal of Mathematical Sociology 1: 49-80.
Lundberg, Ferdinand (1968) The Rich and the Super Rich. New York: Bantam.
——— (1937) America's Sixty Families. New York: Citadel.
McCreary, Edward, Jr., and Walter Guzzardi, Jr. (1965) "A customer is a company's best friend." Fortune (June): 180-194.
Mace, Myles (1971) Directors: Myth and Reality. Cambridge, MA: Harvard University Graduate School of Business Administration.
MacKenzie, Kenneth D. (1966) "Structural centrality in communications networks." Psychometrika 31: 17-25.
MacRae, Duncan, Jr. (1960) "Direct factor analysis of sociometric data." Sociometry 23: 360-371.
March, James G. (1956) "Influence measurement in experimental and semi-experimental groups." Sociometry 19: 260-271.

——— and Herbert A. Simon (1958) Organizations. New York: John Wiley.

Mariolis, Peter (1978) "Bank and financial control of large corporations in the United States." Ph.D. dissertation, SUNY at Stony Brook.

——— (1977) "Type of corporation, size of firm, and interlocking directorates: a reply to Levine." Social Science Quarterly 58: 511-513.

——— (1975) "Interlocking directorates and control of corporations: the theory of bank control." Social Science Quarterly 56: 425-439.

——— Michael Schwartz, and Beth Mintz (1979) "Centrality analysis: a methodology for social networks." Presented at the annual meeting of the American Sociological Association, Boston.

Marris, Robin L. (1964) The Economic Theory of Managerial Capitalism. London: Macmillan.

Means, Gardiner C. (1968) "Implications of the corporate revolution in economic theory," in Adolf A. Berle and Gardiner C. Means, The Modern Corporation and Private Property. New York: Harcourt Brace Jovanovich.

Menshikov, S. (1969) Millionaires and Managers. Moscow: Progress Publishers.

Miliband, Ralph (1969) The State in Capitalist Society. New York: Basic Books.

Mills, C. Wright (1956) The Power Elite. New York: Oxford University Press.

Mintz, Beth (1978) "Who controls the corporation?: a study of interlocking directorates." Ph.D. dissertation, SUNY at Stony Brook.

——— (1975) "The President's Cabinet, 1897-1972: a contribution to the power structure debate." Insurgent Sociologist 5: 131-148.

——— and Michael Schwartz (forthcoming) Bank Hegemony, Corporate Networks, and Intercorporate Power.

——— (1980) "The structure of power in American business." Revision of a paper presented at the annual meeting of the American Political Science Association, Washington, D.C., September 1977. (unpublished)

Mitchell, J. Clyde (1969) "The concept and use of social networks," in J. Clyde Mitchell (ed.) Social Networks in Urban Situations. Manchester: Manchester University Press.

Mizruchi, Mark S. and David Bunting (1981) "Influence in corporate networks: an examination of four measures." Administrative Science Quarterly 26: 475-489.

Mokken, R. J. and F. N. Stokman (1979) "Corporate-governmental networks in the Netherlands." Social Networds 1: 333-358.

Monsen, R. Joseph, Jr., J. S. Chiu, and D. E. Cooley (1965) "The effect of separation of ownership and control on the performance of the large firm." Quarterly Journal of Economics 82: 435-451.

Moody, John (1919) The Masters of Capital. New Haven, CT: Yale University Press.

Moore, Thomas (1980) "Class structure and orientation to work." Presented at the annual meeting of the Eastern Sociological Society, Boston.

Moreno, J. L. (1953) Who Shall Survive? Beacon, NY: Beacon House.

Nemenyi, Peter (1978) "Linear hypotheses—multiple comparisons," in William Kruskal and Judith M. Tanur (eds.) International Encyclopedia of Statistics. New York: Free Press.

Nieminen, Juhari (1973) "On the centrality in a directed graph." Social Science Research 2: 371-378.

Noyes, Alexander D. (1909) Forty Years of American Finance. New York: G. P. Putnam.

O'Connor, James (1972) "Question: Who rules the corporations? Answer: The ruling class." Socialist Revolution 7: 117-150.

––– (1968) "Finance capital or corporate capital?" Monthly Review 20: 30-35.

Palmer, Donald (1979) "Broken ties: some political and interorganizational determinants of interlocking directorates among large American corporations." M.A. thesis, SUNY at Stony Brook.

Palmer, John (1973) "The profit-performance effects of the separation of ownership from control in large United States corporations." Bell Journal of Economics and Management Science 4: 293-303.

Parsons, Talcott (1968) "The distribution of power in American society," in G. William Domhoff and Hoyt Ballard (eds.) C. Wright Mills and the Power Elite. Boston: Beacon.

––– and Neil Smelser (1957) Economy and Society. London: Routledge & Kegan Paul.

Patman Committee (1968) Commercial Banks and Their Trust Activities: Emerging Influence on the American Economy. Washington, DC: Government Printing Office.

Pecora, Ferdinand (1939) Wall Street Under Oath. New York: Simon & Schuster.

Pennings, Johannes M. (1980) Interlocking Directorates. San Francisco: Jossey-Bass.

Perlo, Victor (1957) The Empire of High Finance. New York: International.

Perrow, Charles (1979) Complex Organizations: A Critical Essay. Chicago: Scott, Foresman.

––– (1976) "Control in organizations: the centralized-decentralized bureaucracy." Presented at the annual meeting of the American Sociological Association, New York.

Perrucci, Robert and Marc Pilisuk (1970) "Leaders and ruling elites: the interorganizational bases of community power." American Sociological Review 35: 1040-1056.

Pfeffer, Jeffrey (1972) "Size and composition of corporate boards of directors." Administrative Science Quarterly 17: 218-228.

––– and Phillip Nowak (1976) "Joint ventures and interorganizational interdependence." Administrative Science Quarterly 21: 398-418.

Pfeffer, Jeffrey and Gerald R. Salancik (1978) The External Control of Organizations: A Resource Dependence Perspective. New York: Harper & Row.

Pratt, Soreno S. (1904) "Who owns the United States?" World's Work 17: 4259-4266.

Prewitt, Kenneth and Alan Stone (1973) The Ruling Elites. New York: Harper & Row.

Pujo Committee [U.S. Congress, House Banking and Currency Committee] (1913) Investigation of Concentration of Control of Money and Credit. Washington, DC: Government Printing Office.

Ratcliff, Richard E. (1980) "Banks and corporate lending: an analysis of the impact of the internal structure of the capitalist class on the lending behavior of banks." American Sociological Review 45: 553-570.

––– Kay Oehler, and Mark Gallops (1979) "Networks of financial power: an analysis of the impact of the internal structure of the capitalist class on the lending behavior of banks." Presented at the annual meeting of the American Sociological Association, Boston.

Redlich, Fritz (1951) The Molding of American Banking: Men and Ideas, Vol. II. New York: Hafner.

Ricci, David (1971) Community Power and Democratic Theory. New York: Random House.

Riesman, David (1953) The Lonely Crowd. Garden City, NY: Anchor.

Rochester, Anna (1936) Rulers of America. New York: International.

Rogers, David L. and Meridean L. Maas (1979) "Indicators of organizational power: a comparative analysis involving public and private organizations." Presented at the annual meeting of the American Sociological Association, Boston.

Rose, Arnold (1967) The Power Structure. New York: Oxford University Press.

Roy, William G. (1981) "The unfolding of the interlocking directorate structure of the United States." Department of Sociology, University of California–Los Angeles. (unpublished)

——— "Inter-industry vesting of interests in a national polity over time: the United States, 1886-1905." Ph.D. dissertation, University of Michigan.

Sallach, David L. (1974) "Class domination and ideological hegemony." Sociological Quarterly 15: 38-50.

Salzman, Harold and G. William Domhoff (1980) "Corporations, the civic sector, and government: Do they interlock?" Insurgent Sociologist 9: 121-135.

Scott, John P. (1979) Corporations, Classes, and Capitalism. London: Hutchinson.

Schumpeter, Joseph (1942) Capitalism, Socialism, and Democracy. New York: Harper & Row.

Selznick, Philip (1949) TVA and the Grass Roots. New York: Harper & Row.

Seybold, Peter J. (1978) "The development of American political sociology." Ph.D. dissertation, SUNY at Stony Brook.

Sheehan, Robert J. (1967) "Proprietors in the world of big business." Fortune (June 15): 178-183, 242.

Simmel, Georg (1950) "Quantitative aspects of the group," in Kurt Wolff (ed.) The Sociology of Georg Simmel. New York: Free Press.

Simon, Herbert A. (1957) Administrative Behavior. New York: Macmillan.

Sobel, Robert (1965) The Big Board. New York: Free Press.

Sonquist, John A. and Tom Koenig (1976) "Examining corporate interconnections through interlocking directorates," in Tom R. Burns and Walter Buckley (eds.) Power and Control: Social Structures and Their Transformation. Beverly Hills, CA: Sage.

Soref, Michael (1976) "Social class and a division of labor within the corporate elite." Sociological Quarterly 17: 360-368.

Stanworth, Philip and Anthony Giddens (1975) "The modern corporate economy: interlocking directorates in Britain, 1906-1970." Sociological Review 23: 5-28.

Stigler, George J. (1968) The Organization of Industry. Homewood, IL: Irwin.

Strodtbeck, Fred L. (1954) "The family as a three-person group." American Sociological Review 19: 23-29.

Sweezy, Paul M. (1972) "The resurgence of financial control: fact or fancy?" in Paul M. Sweezy and Harry Magdoff, The Dynamics of U.S. Capitalism. New York: Monthly Review Press.

——— (1953) "Interest groups in the American economy," in Paul M. Sweezy (ed.) The Present as History. New York: Monthly Review Press. (Originally published as the appendix to National Resources Committee, The Structure of the American Economy, 1939.)

――― (1941) "The decline of the investment banker." Antioch Review 1: 63-68.

――― and Harry Magdoff (1975) "Banks: skating on thin ice." Monthly Review 26: 1-21.

Temporary National Economic Committee [TNEC] (1940) The Distribution of Ownership in the 200 Largest Nonfinancial Corporations. Monograph 29. Washington, DC: Government Printing Office.

Thibaut, John W. and Harold H. Kelley (1959) The Social Psychology of Groups. New York: John Wiley.

Thompson, James D. and William J. McEwen (1958) "Organizational goals and environment: goal-setting as an interaction process." American Sociological Review 23: 23-31.

Travers, A. H., Jr. (1968) "Interlocks in corporate management and the antitrust laws." Texas Law Review 46: 819-864.

Useem, Michael (1980) "Corporations and the corporate elite." Annual Review of Sociology 6: 41-77.

――― (1979) "The social organization of the American business elite and participation of corporate directors in the governance of American institutions." American Sociological Review 44: 553-572.

Vance, Stanley C. (1968) The Corporate Director. Homewood, IL: Dow Jones-Irwin.

Villarejo, Don (1961) Stock Ownership and Control of Corporations. Somerville, MA: New England Free Press.

Warner, W. Lloyd and Darab Unwalla (1967) "The system of interlocking directorates," in W. L. Warner, D. Unwalla, and J. Trimm (eds.) The Emergent American Society, Vol. I. New Haven, CT: Yale University Press.

Weber, Max (1968) Economy and Society (Guenther Roth and Claus Wittich, eds.). New York: Bedminster.

White, Harrison C., Scott A. Boorman, and Ronald L. Breiger (1976) "Social structure from multiple networks—Part I: Blockmodels of roles and positions." American Journal of Sociology 81: 730-780.

Whyte, William Foote (1943) Street Corner Society. Chicago: University of Chicago Press.

Williamson, Oliver (1964) The Economics of Discretionary Behavior: Managerial Objectives in a Theory of the Firm. Englewood Cliffs, NJ: Prentice-Hall.

Wright, Erik Olin and Luca Perrone (1977) "Marxist class categories and income inequality." American Sociological Review 42: 34-57.

Youngman, Anna (1907) "The tendency of modern combination." Journal of Political Economy 15: 193-208, 284-298.

Zald, Mayer N. (1969) "The power and function of boards of directors: a theoretical synthesis." American Journal of Sociology 75: 97-111.

Zeitlin, Maurice (1974) "Corporate ownership and control: the large corporation and the capitalist class." American Journal of Sociology 79: 1073-1119.

INDEX

ABOUT THE AUTHOR

MARK S. MIZRUCHI is a Statistical Analyst in the Scientific Computing Center, Albert Einstein College of Medicine, New York. He received his Ph.D. at the State University of New York–Stony Brook in 1980. He is the author of a number of articles on intercorporate relations and coauthor of two forthcoming books, *The Corporate Elite as a Ruling Class* (Holmes & Meier) and *Structural Analysis of Business* (Academic Press).